A Retreat With
Brother Lawrence and the Russian Pilgrim

Other titles in the A Retreat With... *Series:*

Our Lady of Guadalupe and Juan Diego: Heeding the Call, by Virgilio Elizondo and Friends

Our Lady, Dominic and Ignatius: Praying With Our Bodies, by Betsey Beckman, Nina O'Connor and J. Michael Sparough, S.J.

Patrick: Discovering God in All, by Timothy Joyce, O.S.B.

Pope John XXIII: Opening the Windows to Wisdom, by Alfred McBride, O. Praem.

Teresa of Avila: Living by Holy Wit, by Gloria Hutchinson

Thea Bowman and Bede Abram: Leaning On the Lord, by Joseph A. Brown, S.J.

Therese of Lisieux: Loving Our Way Into Holiness, by Elizabeth Ruth Obbard, O.D.C.

Thomas Merton: Becoming Who We Are, by Dr. Anthony T. Padovano

A RETREAT WITH
BROTHER LAWRENCE AND
THE RUSSIAN PILGRIM

Praying Ceaselessly

Kerry Walters

ST. ANTHONY MESSENGER PRESS

Cincinnati, Ohio

& Schuster, *A Diary of Private Prayer*, by John Baillie, copyright ©1949. Reprinted by permission of ICS Publications, *The Selected Poetry...*, by Jessica Powers, Regina Siegfried and Robert Morneau, eds., copyright ©1989. Reprinted by permission of The University of Chicago Press, *The Prayers of Kierkegaard*, Perry D. LeFevre, ed., copyright ©1963.

Cover illustration by Steve Erspamer, S.M.
Cover and book design by Mary Alfieri
Electronic format and pagination by Sandy L. Digman

ISBN 0-86716-369-0

Published by St. Anthony Messenger Press
Printed in the U.S.A.

DEDICATION

*For the good people
of St. Andrew's*

Contents

Introducing A Retreat With...

Twenty years ago I made a weekend retreat at a Franciscan house on the coast of New Hampshire. The retreat director's opening talk was as lively as a long-range weather forecast. He told us how completely God loves each one of us—without benefit of lively anecdotes or fresh insights.

As the friar rambled on, my inner critic kept up a *sotto voce* commentary: "I've heard all this before." "Wish he'd say something new that I could chew on." "That poor man really doesn't have much to say." Ever hungry for manna yet untasted, I devalued any experience of hearing the same old thing.

After a good night's sleep, I awoke feeling as peaceful as a traveler who has at last arrived safely home. I walked across the room toward the closet. On the way I passed the sink with its small framed mirror on the wall above. Something caught my eye like an unexpected presence. I turned, saw the reflection in the mirror and said aloud, "No wonder he loves me!"

This involuntary affirmation stunned me. What or whom had I seen in the mirror? When I looked again, it was "just me," an ordinary person with a lower-than-average reservoir of self-esteem. But I knew that in the initial vision I had seen God-in-me breaking through like a sudden sunrise.

At that moment I knew what it meant to be made in the divine image. I understood right down to my size eleven feet what it meant to be loved exactly as I was.

Only later did I connect this revelation with one granted to the Trappist monk-writer Thomas Merton. As he reports in *Conjectures of a Guilty Bystander*, while standing all unsuspecting on a street corner one day, he was overwhelmed by the "joy of being...a member of a race in which God Himself became incarnate.... There is no way of telling people that they are all walking around shining like the sun."

As an absentminded homemaker may leave a wedding ring on the kitchen windowsill, so I have often mislaid this precious conviction. But I have never forgotten that particular retreat. It persuaded me that the Spirit rushes in where it will. Not even a boring director or a judgmental retreatant can withstand the "violent wind" that "fills the entire house" where we dwell in expectation (see Acts 2:2).

So why deny ourselves any opportunity to come aside awhile and rest on holy ground? Why not withdraw from the daily web that keeps us muddled and wound? Wordsworth's complaint is ours as well: "The world is too much with us." There is no flu shot to protect us from infection by the skepticism of the media, the greed of commerce, the alienating influence of technology. We need retreats as the deer needs the running stream.

An Invitation

This book and its companions in the *A Retreat With...* series from St. Anthony Messenger Press are designed to meet that need. They are an invitation to choose as director some of the most powerful, appealing and wise mentors our faith tradition has to offer.

Our directors come from many countries, historical eras and schools of spirituality. At times they are teamed to sing in close harmony (for example, Francis de Sales, Jane de Chantal and Aelred of Rievaulx on spiritual friendship). Others are paired to kindle an illuminating fire from the friction of their differing views (such as Augustine of Hippo and Mary Magdalene on human sexuality). All have been chosen because, in their humanness and their holiness, they can help us grow in self-knowledge, discernment of God's will and maturity in the Spirit.

Inviting us into relationship with these saints and holy ones are inspired authors from today's world, women and men whose creative gifts open our windows to the Spirit's flow. As a motto for the authors of our series, we have borrowed the advice of Dom Frederick Dunne to the young Thomas Merton. Upon joining the Trappist monks, Merton wanted to sacrifice his writing activities lest they interfere with his contemplative vocation. Dom Frederick wisely advised, "Keep on writing books that make people love the spiritual life."

That is our motto. Our purpose is to foster (or strengthen) friendships between readers and retreat directors —friendships that feed the soul with wisdom, past and present. Like the scribe "trained for the kingdom of heaven," each author brings forth from his or her storeroom "what is new and what is old" (Matthew 13:52).

The Format

The pattern for each *A Retreat With...* remains the same; readers of one will be in familiar territory when they move on to the next. Each book is organized as a seven-session retreat that readers may adapt to their own schedules or to the needs of a group.

Day One begins with an anecdotal introduction called

"Getting to Know Our Directors." Readers are given a telling glimpse of the guides with whom they will be sharing the retreat experience. A second section, "Placing Our Directors in Context," will enable retreatants to see the guides in their own historical, geographical, cultural and spiritual settings.

Having made the human link between seeker and guide, the authors go on to "Introducing Our Retreat Theme." This section clarifies how the guide(s) are especially suited to explore the theme and how the retreatant's spirituality can be nourished by it.

After an original "Opening Prayer" to breathe life into the day's reflection, the author, speaking with and through the mentor(s), will begin to spin out the theme. While focusing on the guide(s)' own words and experience, the author may also draw on Scripture, tradition, literature, art, music, psychology or contemporary events to illuminate the path.

Each day's session is followed by reflection questions designed to challenge, affirm and guide the reader in integrating the theme into daily life. A "Closing Prayer" brings the session full circle and provides a spark of inspiration for the reader to harbor until the next session.

Days Two through Six begin with "Coming Together in the Spirit" and follow a format similar to Day One. Day Seven weaves the entire retreat together, encourages a continuation of the mentoring relationship and concludes with "Deepening Your Acquaintance," an envoi to live the theme by God's grace, the director(s)' guidance and the retreatant's discernment. A closing section of Resources serves as a larder from which readers may draw enriching books, videos, cassettes and films.

We hope readers will experience at least one of those memorable "No wonder God loves me!" moments. And we hope that they will have "talked back" to the mentors, as good friends are wont to do.

A case in point: There was once a famous preacher who always drew a capacity crowd to the cathedral. Whenever he spoke, an eccentric old woman sat in the front pew directly beneath the pulpit. She took every opportunity to mumble complaints and contradictions— just loud enough for the preacher to catch the drift that he was not as wonderful as he was reputed to be. Others seated down front glowered at the woman and tried to shush her. But she went right on needling the preacher to her heart's content.

When the old woman died, the congregation was astounded at the depth and sincerity of the preacher's grief. Asked why he was so bereft, he responded, "Now who will help me to grow?"

All of our mentors in *A Retreat With...* are worthy guides. Yet none would seek retreatants who simply said, "Where you lead, I will follow. You're the expert." In truth, our directors provide only half the retreat's content. Readers themselves will generate the other half.

As general editor for the retreat series, I pray that readers will, by their questions, comments, doubts and decision-making, fertilize the seeds our mentors have planted.

And may the Spirit of God rush in to give the growth.

Gloria Hutchinson
Series Editor
Conversion of Saint Paul, 1995

Getting to Know Our Directors

Our two retreat directors, Brother Lawrence and the Russian Pilgrim, come from different times and places, and they speak different languages. One, bound by a religious vow of stability, spent the greater part of his life serving God in a monastic enclosure. The other, prodded by deep spiritual wanderlust, roamed for years over steppes and forests and through villages and towns in search of God. One drew sustenance from western Catholicism, the other from eastern Orthodoxy. One served as a soldier and witnessed firsthand the brutality of war. The other, although spared this horror, was nonetheless a victim of violent hatred and envy. One remained single and probably celibate his entire life. The other married and for a while knew the joy of erotic love.

Underneath their different backgrounds, however, is a shared spiritual center of gravity. Both Brother Lawrence and the Russian Pilgrim believed and taught that the scriptural injunction to pray unceasingly (for example, 1 Thessalonians 5:17) is a realistic goal for all God-seekers, not a state of grace reserved only for cloistered religious or saints. Although genuine prayer always and everywhere is a mystery, there's nothing mysterious— much less magical—about the way to cultivate continuous prayer. A method or spiritual discipline is, by God's grace, available to everyone. One of our retreat directors, Brother Lawrence, calls this discipline "practicing the presence of God." The Russian Pilgrim, our second director, refers to it as "self-activating prayer of the heart."

As we'll see over the course of our week-long journey into prayer, one of the consequences of praying ceaselessly is that we normally self-absorbed creatures gradually wean ourselves away from our intoxication with ego, or the false self. Our worldly identities, characterized by criss-crossing ambitions, desires and jealousies, begin to peel away as the discipline of ceaseless prayer sinks ever deeper into our hearts. We shuck off the old self which previously demanded all our time and attention in order to make room for God, and in the process we discover the Christ-self, our true identity. We decrease so that God may increase—so that, in the words of the apostle Paul, it is Christ rather than the false self who lives in us.[1]

Given that the goal of ceaseless prayer is to de-emphasize the self, it seems fitting that we know so little about the lives of our two retreat directors. Their teachings on prayer come down through the years to us with undiminished clarity. But their own biographies have receded into the duskiness of near anonymity, as if to remind us that what's important is not the messenger but the message. Brother Lawrence and the Pilgrim wish us to focus on God, the Alpha and Omega, not on themselves. They decreased so that God might increase.

This, of course, is as it should be. Still, it will be helpful for those of us on retreat to be able to put faces on our spiritual directors, even though the features must remain vague. If we coax Brother Lawrence and the Russian Pilgrim from the shadows, we can discover something—although, again, not much—about the sorts of persons they are.

Introducing Brother Lawrence

Chances are good Brother Lawrence would insist that there's only one bit of information about his personal life worth passing on to others. He himself shared it with Abbé Joseph de Beaufort, the superior of the Parisian monastery where Brother Lawrence was a professed lay brother. It's the story of his conversion, which occurred when he was eighteen. Here is de Beaufort's retelling:

> One day in winter, while looking at a tree stripped of its leaves, and reflecting that after a time its leaves would appear again and then flowers and fruits, [Brother Lawrence] received a lofty view of the providence and the power of God which has never been effaced from his soul. This view drew him altogether from the world, and gave him such a love for God that he was unable to say whether it had increased during the span of forty years since he had received this grace.[2]

There are certain moments of *kairos*, of grace-sparked opportunity for spiritual insight and growth, in every person's life. Often these moments go unnoticed because for one reason or another the individual isn't ready for them. A person accustomed to a diet of bread and milk can't be expected to digest more solid fare easily. But sometimes life experience and *kairos* intersect at just the right instant, and when this happens the individual's life is converted (literally, "turned") in a new direction.

Such a kairetic moment of turning caught up with Brother Lawrence when he was eighteen. Fortunately, we can piece together enough of his biography prior to his conversion to get some idea of why the accidental sight of a winter-blasted tree was a transformative revelation for him.

We don't know the exact year of Brother Lawrence's birth—possibilities range from 1608 to 1614—but we do know the location: Héremini (or Herimesnil) in France's Lorraine district. He was christened Nicolas Herman and lived with his parents, both of whom seem to have been conventionally religious, until his mid to late teens. Sometime just prior to his conversion experience, young Nicolas joined the Lorraine army and fought in a handful of battles in what became known as the Thirty Years War. This chapter in his life was brief but horrific. He was captured and accused of spying, and narrowly escaped hanging. Finally released, he was soon wounded in a skirmish and sent home to recuperate. His military career was finished scarcely before it began.

Nicolas's short but intense war experience served as the catalyst for the revelation (which presumably took place during his convalescence) in the winter orchard. The war had forced him at least twice into urgent confrontations with his own mortality. Moreover, young Nicolas probably had witnessed or at least heard about the horrible atrocities that were all too standard in the European conflict that had swept him up. All wars at best are stupid and brutal, but religious wars are especially so since each side believes—or pretends to believe—that it has a divine mandate which absolves excesses. The Thirty Years War was one of the worst of the many religious conflicts which stain the history of European Christianity. Civilians were routinely robbed, raped and murdered; town and countryside were ravaged. The mayhem continued for an entire generation.

Fresh from this nightmare, weakened by his wounds and dark memories, Nicolas must have felt that his young life was as blighted and desolate as the bare trees outside his window. But by the grace of God, the wind of hope and faith blew through his inner landscape and Nicolas experienced a great spiritual truth. The seed which falls to the ground and dies does so only as a prelude to rebirth. ◗

He knew that the divine love which resurrects trees each spring would likewise revive and sustain his wounded soul.

Like so many who experience conversion, Nicolas wasn't quite sure what to do with his new life. After his recovery he became footman for a time to William de Fuibet, treasurer of Louis XIII. His service, however, was short-lived. Probably his heart wasn't in it; besides, as he later admitted, he'd been a "big heavy-handed fellow who broke everything."[3] He thought about joining a monastery, but then decided to try the life of a religious hermit. This, too, proved unsuccessful, but at least it taught Nicolas that he needed the practical and spiritual discipline of an established order to help him grow in the service of God. At last in 1640 he requested admission as a lay brother to the Discalced Carmelite monastery on Rue de Vaugirard in Paris. He was accepted, given the name Lawrence of the Resurrection and, two years later, professed. Nicolas Herman, henceforth Brother Lawrence, had finally found the way to live his calling.

The rest of Brother Lawrence's life was outwardly unremarkable. He dwelt in the monastery on the Rue de Vaugirard for another half century, following the strict daily schedule of a professed Carmelite. He remained a lay brother, and a particularly humble one at that. His assigned tasks were all menial: For many years he worked in the monastery kitchen and then, when lamed by gout, in the cobbler's shop. Contemporary descriptions that have come down to us ascribe a rough exterior to Brother Lawrence—Bishop Fénelon goes so far as to say he was "gross by nature"—and there's no surviving evidence that he had scholarly or bookish inclinations. The rawboned and clumsy youth who had fumbled his service to the Duc de Fuibet grew up to be an equally clumsy man.

But shining through Brother Lawrence's rough exterior was a holiness that steadily impressed first his fellow Carmelites and then the world beyond the monastery walls. The same Fénelon who observed that Brother Lawrence was gross by nature summed up the impressions of countless visitors when he hastened to add that the monk was also "delicate by grace." A growing number of people, many of them from the ranks of secular and ecclesial aristocracy, sought out this humble monk for spiritual counsel. Even more corresponded with him. But only sixteen of Lawrence's own letters of instruction have survived. Along with a handful of fragmentary meditations, they are the sum total of his writings which have come down to us. All else we know of his spiritual teaching are transcriptions of conversations between him and the Abbé de Beaufort.

What was it about this unglamorous monk which attracted so much attention? The answer is simple, even if a full appreciation of it is not. Brother Lawrence discovered, lived and taught a spirituality of the presence of God in everyday life. His life attests that the union with God which is the human heart's deepest desire is indeed possible, and his writings and conversations outlined a practical technique for attaining it. The two essential conditions for achieving an ongoing intimacy with God are abandonment and loving mindfulness, both of which we'll explore in our week of retreat. Continuous practice of the presence of God—or, as Saint Paul put it, ceaseless prayer—occurs when we *abandon* our self-will for the sake of the divine will and *discipline* our hearts and minds to be ever *mindful* of God's immediacy in our lives and in the world. At the end of the day, the interior gaze which focuses lovingly on God is a divinely bestowed grace. But we can certainly make ourselves worthy of the gift by striving for ceaseless prayer in our day-to-day existence, ever assured, as Brother Lawrence tells us, that "God never fails to offer his grace at every juncture."[4] ✗

Introducing the Russian Pilgrim

Travel some two centuries and several hundred miles east from Brother Lawrence's time and country and you meet an even more shadowy spiritual mentor—the second of our two retreat directors. He appears on the historical horizon for a brief instant of time and just as enigmatically recedes back into oblivion. It's not clear exactly when he lived, although the second half of the nineteenth century is as good a guess as any, and we don't even know his name. We call him simply the "Russian Pilgrim." He referred to himself as a "homeless wanderer":

> By the grace of God I am a Christian man, by actions a great sinner, and by calling a homeless wanderer of the humblest birth who roams from place to place. My worldly goods are a knapsack with some dried bread in it on my back, and in my breastpocket a Bible. And that is all.[5]

The Russian Pilgrim was a wandering God-seeker, one of thousands of itinerant men and women who traveled the highways and byways of imperial Russia, roaming from one monastery to the next in search of a *starets* or *skhimnitsa*—a monk or nun celebrated for holiness—who could provide spiritual direction. Some Russians were leery of religious pilgrims, and tended to dismiss them as mountebanks or lunatics. The Russian Pilgrim himself ran across several such skeptics.[6] But for the most part, religious itinerants were viewed as saints touched by the Holy Spirit and treated with respect and generosity in the towns and villages through which they passed.

The Pilgrim who serves as the codirector of our retreat was unusual among holy itinerants in that he could both read *and* write. Many of his fellow pilgrims were able to pick their way through the Gospels, but few knew how to write. Consequently, almost all the accounts of them which have survived are secondhand. But the Russian Pilgrim penned a memoir of his geographical and spiritual odysseys.[7] The one took him through vast regions of western and central Russia. The other led him into the heart of ceaseless interior prayer.

The Russian Pilgrim was born in the vicinity of Orel, a city two hundred miles due south of Moscow. Orphaned at the age of two, he and his ten-year-old brother were adopted by their grandfather. The old man, whom the Russian Pilgrim describes with tender affection, was a comfortably successful innkeeper who knew his Bible, attended church regularly and treated indigent travelers generously. But the Pilgrim's elder brother was another matter entirely. A madcap child who grew into a sullen youth, the brother took to drink at an early age and began a whirlwind descent into violence and debauchery. But dissolute and shameful though he was, he's also responsible in at least two ways for the fact that the Russian Pilgrim is codirector of our retreat.

First, the elder brother was the indirect cause of the Pilgrim's literacy, and hence of his written spiritual counsels to us. When the Pilgrim was seven years old his brother pushed him so violently that his left arm was severely broken and subsequently withered up. As time passed and the arm failed to heal, the Pilgrim's grandfather realized that the lad would never be fit for physical labor. So he taught the boy to read, and hired a local clerk to teach him how to write as well.

Second, the elder brother was also the brutal catalyst

for the Russian Pilgrim's decision to take to the road in search of God. When the Pilgrim was seventeen, his grandfather arranged a marriage for him. Soon afterwards the grandfather himself died, leaving the inn and all his money to the Pilgrim and his bride. "Obey your conscience, deceive no one, and above all pray to God," was the old man's final advice. "Everything comes from God. Trust in Him only."[8]

But the rapscallion elder brother was furious at the old man's disinheritance of him, and one drunken night changed the Pilgrim's life forever. He broke into the inn while everyone slept, stole the inherited money and then set fire to the building. The Pilgrim and his wife only just managed to escape with the nightclothes on their backs. Everything else was lost in the blaze. The elder brother, along with the inheritance, disappeared without a trace.

The Pilgrim and his wife lived for the next two years in grinding poverty. They managed to piece together a hovel to keep out rain and snow, but otherwise were quite destitute. The Pilgrim was unable to work because of his useless left arm; his wife brought in what few rubles she could through needlework. But the wretched life proved too much for her, and she eventually sickened and died. The widowed Pilgrim sold the hut and all his possessions except for his grandfather's Bible. Then he took to the road. He was only twenty years old.

Although the Pilgrim is reticent about his motive for taking up the wandering life, a likely explanation is close at hand. Like Brother Lawrence, the Pilgrim had suffered a grievous psychological and spiritual trauma. In the space of two years he lost his grandfather, his livelihood, his prospects and his wife. Betrayal, treachery, blind envy, hatred: The Pilgrim was the innocent victim of each of these poisonous passions. His own flesh and blood revealed to him the vile depths to which humans can sink. And all the while, his grandfather's dying words constantly echoed in his ears: "...above all pray to God; everything comes from Him. Trust in Him only." But the words which once inspired now only mocked: How could God have allowed such suffering to fall upon an innocent man? It is a question as old as Job.

The Russian Pilgrim set out in search of an answer. He shouldered the rucksack of a religious itinerant because he knew he was spiritually damaged and needed the healing power of a *starets* to make him whole again. Like the ancient Hebrews, he took to the wilderness to rediscover God.

Brother Lawrence's breakthrough occurred one bleak winter day as he gazed at a wind-stripped tree. The Russian Pilgrim tells us that his own kairetic moment fell on the twenty-fourth Sunday after Pentecost (we don't know the year). On that morning, he says,

> I went to church to say my prayers there during the liturgy. The first Epistle of St. Paul to the Thessalonians was being read, and among other words I heard these—'Pray without ceasing.' It was this text, more than any other, which forced itself upon my mind, and I began to think how it was possible to pray without ceasing, since a man has to concern himself with other things also in order to make a living. I looked at my Bible and with my own eyes read the words which I had heard, that is, that we ought always, at all times and in all places, to pray with uplifted hands. I thought and thought, but knew not what to make of it.[9]

The naked winter tree brought home to Brother Lawrence the great truth that the spirit resurrects even in the midst of decay and desolation. The gospel injunction to pray ceaselessly awakened in the Russian Pilgrim the trust that abiding communion with a loving God is possible. Both

experiences seem absurd catalysts: a frostbitten tree
surely isn't an obvious emblem of rebirth, and the
prospect of ceaseless prayer "at all times and in all
places,...with uplifted hands" is so impractical that it's
difficult to take literally. But what seems foolish in the
eyes of the world is frequently wisdom in God's.

The Russian Pilgrim now had a lodestar by which to
steer his course. He began visiting churches and
monasteries in search of someone who could teach him
how to pray ceaselessly. But he had no success. Everyone
he met recommended continuous prayer as a means of
uniting with God, but no one actually knew *how* to pray
ceaselessly.

Finally, however, his perseverance paid off. The
Russian Pilgrim located a *starets* who taught him that
ceaseless prayer is not a matter of words and uplifted
hands but of silence and uplifted heart. Ceaseless prayer
is an interior movement of the spirit toward God, a
mindfulness of God's constant presence, a stretching of
the soul toward the divine. And the *starets* provided the
Pilgrim with a method for learning how to pray
ceaselessly: the Jesus prayer. There are several varieties of
this prayer, but the one used and in turn taught by the
Russian Pilgrim is "Lord Jesus Christ, have mercy on
me." Repeated constantly, first with the lips, then with the
mind, the point is to make the prayer such an intimate
part of one's existence that at last it sinks into the heart
and takes on a life of its own—becomes, in the Pilgrim's
words, "self-activating." When this happens, one prays
ceaselessly—or, better, one *becomes* a ceaseless prayer. This
is the great spiritual insight the Russian Pilgrim learned,
and it is what he shares with us on this retreat.

A final word about our two spiritual guides by way
of introduction: Please don't think of them as plaster-cast
saints or other-worldly ascetics who piously raise their

eyes to a heaven inaccessible to the rest of us. Brother
Lawrence and the Russian Pilgrim are persons, just like
you and me. They are fragile, vulnerable humans who
suffered trauma, despair, confusion, anger and doubt—
also like you and me. Their spiritual fervor as well as
their progress ebbed and flowed; they did not float easily
down the river of grace—again, like most of us. This is
why Brother Lawrence and the Russian Pilgrim are
trustworthy retreat directors. The insights they share with
us about ceaseless prayer and union with God were
learned from the school of life, not from the abstract
study of theology books. They speak to us where we are,
because they've been there themselves. They are our
mentors because they were first our fellow-travelers.

Placing Our Directors in Context

In the preface to his *Seeds of Contemplation*, Thomas
Merton claims that his spiritual reflections are not
"revolutionary or even especially original." The only
thing new about them, he says, is their mode of
presentation. The style is his, but the insights belong to
the great Christian contemplative tradition. He is simply
tapping into that tradition and translating it into
contemporary language.[10]

Merton's self-appraisal is a good litmus test for all
spiritual and devotional writing. The point is not so much
to come up with something new.[11] The ideals and
principles of the spiritual life remain constant. Instead,
the task is to cast new light upon tried and tested truths
so that they reveal themselves in verbal and imaginative
symbols each successive generation can appreciate. When
this happens, the recast spiritual insights (in spite of
Merton's modest disclaimer) can indeed provoke a

revolutionary awakening in the human heart.

Our two retreat directors are adepts at breathing life into ancient spiritual truths. Neither of them offer "original" reflections. Their teachings flow from two devotional traditions which are ultimately based in Scripture. In Brother Lawrence's case, that tradition is Carmelite spirituality; with the Russian Pilgrim, it is orthodox hesychasm. But the manner in which Brother Lawrence and the Russian Pilgrim express the insights gleaned from their respective spiritual contexts is both revelatory and revolutionary: revelatory in that it opens our eyes to dimensions of prayer which hitherto may have been hidden from us, and revolutionary in that it is capable of forever changing our lives. In following their direction, we rediscover and embrace the biblical ideal of ceaseless interior prayer.

Brother Lawrence's Spiritual World

The Carmelite order to which Brother Lawrence belonged claimed to have been founded in pre-Jesus days as an eremitical religious community, and thus styled itself Christendom's oldest monastic order. Less fancifully, it appears to have gotten its start in the early twelfth century when a handful of crusaders established themselves as religious hermits atop Mount Carmel.

Ambiguous though the order's historical origins may be, what has never been in doubt is the contemplative nature of Carmelite spirituality. From the very beginning, the order emphasized the centrality of interior prayer, silence and solitude in the spiritual development of its members. The goal was to wean the heart from selfish desires and the mind from worldly distractions so that the aspirant could focus exclusively on God. In pursuit of this God-centered end, Carmelites became notorious for their strict rule and severe asceticism.

As is the nature of such things, the austerity of the Carmelite rule relaxed over the two centuries following the order's founding, partly through official decree, partly out of unofficial laxness. But in the middle of the sixteenth century a couple of prophets appeared who reformed the Carmelite order and taught a spirituality which served as the context for Brother Lawrence's practice of the presence of God one hundred years later. These two great mentors were Teresa of Avila (1515-1582) and John of the Cross (1542-1591).

Both Teresa and John led the Carmelites back onto the path of interior prayer. In her spiritual classic *Interior Castle*, Teresa taught that the soul is like a great castle "made of a single diamond or of very clear crystal."[12] This castle has many interconnecting chambers or "mansions," and deep within the central chamber is God. If an aspirant would discover God, she must travel through the rooms of her interior castle, one by one, progressively abandoning self-will, until she finally works her way to the center wherein God resides. In *The Way of Perfection* as well as in the middle chapters of her delightful autobiography, Teresa teaches a four-step method of prayer to help the God-seeker make this interior journey. The method begins with oral, discursive prayer and moves gradually to a silent, contemplative union with the divine. Teresa promised that although prayerful union with God may initially be transitory and sporadic, it becomes more continuous—more *lived*—as the aspirant sinks deeper into the heart of silent interior prayer.

John of the Cross likewise envisioned the route to God as an interior one. God, he tells us, is like a seed buried deeply within the soul. The spiritual journey is a gradually dawning realization that the kingdom of heaven is already within us, and that we are called upon to nurture its growth. Mindfulness is the key here: The aspirant must be ever aware of the presence of God in his life, and resolutely rid himself of all distractions that get in the way of embracing that presence. This turning away from things which are not of God ultimately blossoms into what John refers to sometimes as "spiritual marriage" (*Spiritual Canticle*) and sometimes as "divine union" (*Ascent of Mount Carmel*). It is a loving communion with God, a substitution of Christ for ego, an ongoing interior celebration of the kingdom of heaven.

Brother Lawrence was a lay brother in the Discalced (shoeless) Carmelites, the reformed order founded by Teresa and John, and thus was heavily influenced by their teachings on interior prayer and contemplation. It's not clear if Lawrence had firsthand acquaintance with their writings, but the spiritual milieu of a seventeenth-century discalced monastery would have been steeped in their influence. What's not uncertain at all is the fact that Brother Lawrence's method of practicing the presence of God falls squarely within the spiritual tradition defended by these two great reformers.

The Russian Pilgrim's Spiritual World

While Carmelite spirituality is a child of the Latin Church, the hesychast tradition that provides the context for the Russian Pilgrim's approach to ceaseless prayer belongs to the Greek Church. Two traditions, two idioms; but the spiritualities birthed by each are remarkably similar.

"Hesychasm" is derived from *hesuchia*, the Greek word for "rest" or "repose." It is a spiritual discipline which cultivates continuous prayer as a means of dwelling in God's presence, with prayer understood here as a receptive silence in which the heart rests or reposes in God. (In fact, the literal translation of "pray always" is "come to rest.") The hesychast believes that such restful silence is a necessary condition for the discovery of the Christ-self within. But the first step in this direction is to wean oneself from the noisy distractions which deafen us to the divine silence. As the seventh-century hesychast John Climacus put it, "the beginning of [hesuchia] is to throw off all noise as disturbing for the depth of the soul. And the end of it is not to fear disturbances and to remain insusceptible to them."[13] In order to train the disciple in attentive silence, hesychasm uses the "Jesus prayer," a mantra-like repetitive verse which focuses the disciple's attention away from distractions and towards God. As we've seen, the hope is that what begins as a self-conscious oral exercise will eventually sink into the heart and become an automatic, lived praise of God, unbroken by either thought or word. When this happens the hesychast, as Brother Lawrence would say, practices the presence of God. Or, as the Russian hesychast Theophan the Recluse put it, to pray is to "descend with the mind into the heart, and there stand before the face of the Lord, ever-present, all-seeing, within you."[14]

Silence has always been important to Judeo-Christian spirituality: Elijah encounters God in the quiet eye of the storm, the Psalmist (46:10) enjoins us to be still and know God, and Christ frequently left the noisy crowd to commune with the Father in silent solitude. But the Jesus prayer as a specific technique for achieving silent repose was first developed, it seems, by the desert fathers and mothers during the first centuries of the Church. Evagrios the Solitary taught the method in the mid-fourth century, and when the sixth-century Saint John Cassian visited the desert hermits to learn their spiritual disciplines firsthand, he found the Jesus prayer widely practiced among the adepts he met. The technique especially flourished in the Greek Church, and the fourteenth-century Orthodox saint Gregory Palamas wrote an elaborate theology revolving around the hesychast insight that the cultivation of restful silence reveals Christ within us (cf. 2 Corinthians 13:5).

By the time of the Russian Pilgrim, a rich body of devotional and theological literature about the hesychast practice of the Jesus prayer existed and was collected in an anthology called the *Philokalia* ("love of the good, beautiful, true"). The Russian Pilgrim was introduced to the *Philokalia* by his *starets,* and the spiritual instruction he in turn hands on to us is studded with spiritual counsel from its pages. The only book more valued by the Russian Pilgrim was his grandfather's Bible.

Notes

[1] Galatians 2:20.

[2] Brother Lawrence, *The Practice of the Presence of God*, E. M. Blaiklock, trans. (London: Hodder and Stoughton, 1981), p. 19.

[3] *The Practice of the Presence of God*, p. 19.

[4] *The Practice of the Presence of God*, p. 29.

[5] *The Way of a Pilgrim, and The Pilgrim Continues his Way*, R. M. French, trans. (San Francisco: Harper, 1991), p. 3.

[6] *The Way of a Pilgrim, and The Pilgrim Continues his Way*, e.g., pp. 45-55, 75-76.

[7] *The Way of the Pilgrim* was first published in 1884, in Kazan, Russia.

[8] *The Way of a Pilgrim*, pp. 61-62.

[9] *The Way of a Pilgrim*, p. 3.

[10] Thomas Merton, *Seeds of Contemplation* (New York: New Directions, 1949), p. 10.

[11] C. S. Lewis interestingly discusses "originality" in a Christian context in his "Christianity and Literature," in *The Seeing Eye*, Walter Hooper, ed. (New York: Ballantine, 1967), pp. 1-14.

[12] Teresa of Avila, *Interior Castle*, E. Allison Peers, trans. (Garden City, N.Y.: Image, 1961), p. 28.

[13] John Climacus, *The Ladder of Divine Ascent*, Archimandrite Lazarus Moore, trans. (London: Faber and Faber, 1959), Step 27, p. 237.

[14] Timothy Ware, ed., *The Art of Prayer: An Orthodox Anthology* (London: Faber and Faber, 1966), p. 110.

Day One
Daring to Dive

7/24/08

Introducing Our Retreat Theme

If a still picture is worth a thousand words, a cinematic one is worth ten thousand. Let's begin our retreat by looking at two film clips that speak volumes about prayer. One is from Monty Python's hilarious *The Meaning of Life*. The other is from the much more sober *Priest*.

The Monty Python clip opens with a wide shot of a staid English chapel properly fitted out in seasoned dark oak and arched stained-glass windows. Morning prayer has just begun. A poker-faced lay reader drones his way through an utterly incomprehensible Old Testament lesson, and then the vested priest solemnly rises for prayer. "Let us praise God," he announces in flawless Oxonian tones. A few dozen bored, preoccupied congregants stand and, following the priest's lead, vacantly recite the following prayer:

> O Lord,
> Ooh, you are so big:
> So absolutely huge.
> Gosh, we're all really impressed down here, I can
>   tell you.
> Forgive us, O Lord, for this our dreadful toadying
>   and graceless flattery.

5

But you're so strong and, well, just so super
fantastic!

Cut to the second clip, this time from the movie *Priest*. A
young vicar frenetically paces up and down in his room,
tearing at his hair, sobbing and shouting to a mute
crucifix on the wall. One of his parishioners, a young girl,
has just revealed to him that her father is sexually
abusing her. But the priest is bound by the seal of
confession, and so can't alert the authorities to what's
going on. Ripped apart by the conflict between his moral
duty to the suffering child and his clerical obligation to
honor the sacrament of confession, the priest drops to his
knees before the crucifix and cries out in agony:

> *Do something*! Don't just hang there you smug, idle
> bastard! Do something!... *You* could speak out! You
> were the son of God for god's sake! You could make
> the rules! You were the son of God! I'm not! I'm just
> a priest. I'm just a tuppence, ha'penny priest, and I
> can't take on two thousand years of history!

Most of us probably don't say our morning prayers in
vaulted British chapels or have to worry about the seal of
confession. We're ordinary people who do our bit on
Sunday mornings and holy days and otherwise try to live
reasonably decent lives. But chances are still good that
these two cinematic commentaries on prayer strike
uncomfortably close to home. When we reflect on our
own prayer lives, we see that at times we stand with the
desultory British congregation and at other times shriek
with the desperate young priest.

This is especially disconcerting because we've been
taught from an early age that prayer is a grace-filled
opportunity for communing with God and so ought to be
a joyous thing, an ecstatic eruption of gratitude and
praise and adoration, a heartfelt thanks-offering from the

beloved to the supreme Lover. Ancient wisdom teaches that authentic prayer is so intense that it's only through God's great kindness that the man or woman who prays survives the experience. But the practice typically falls far short of the ideal, doesn't it? We mumble our way through familiar liturgical prayers, our bodies in church but our hearts and minds a thousand miles away. We breathlessly fly through grace at meals, whip through Hail Marys and Paternosters as if they're unpleasant tasks best done quickly, and cross ourselves with such abrupt and abbreviated motions that it appears for all the world like we're absentmindedly swatting flies. Instead of looking forward to our prayerful visits with God, we're apt to think of them as tiresome chores.

Those times when we *are* present during our prayers are often little better. The sad truth is that we probably throw ourselves most fervently into prayer only when we need or want something. We feel guilty about an act done or left undone, and instead of offering up genuine repentance we toady to God with shameless pharisaisms such as those lampooned by Monty Python. We're confronted with moral or spiritual dilemmas and, along with the vicar in *Priest*, we howl at God to put things right for us. When a magical solution isn't instantly forthcoming, we grow petulant and furious, demanding that God come down from his heavenly high horse and do just this one little thing for us. (How many of us have prefaced our prayers with something like "Lord, you know I don't ask you for much...," as if calling in a few celestial chips?)

All too frequently, in short, we pray either mechanically or selfishly. During normal times we go through the motions of prayer without being mindful of what we're about. During times of stress we *are* mindful, but only to implore, cajole, threaten, promise and blackmail God in a desperate attempt to get what we want. There's no joy, no heartfelt gratitude or loving praise, in either case. Nor is there self-forgetfulness. There's only the alternating pattern of yawning indifference on the one hand and the sense of entitlement characteristic of spoiled children on the other.

To our credit, most of us sense that this kind of prayer life is off course. So, periodically, usually at Lent or Advent, we resolve to clean up our act. We immerse ourselves in prayer for a few days or weeks, and in fact may even feel that our relationship with God is undergoing some kind of rejuvenation. But sooner or later we begin to lose steam until eventually our initial zeal gives way to boredom if not outright distaste. Our periodic bingeing on prayer, like all bingeing, can't be sustained, and the pendulum inevitably swings in the opposite direction.

Is it really any surprise, then, that so many Christians pray in only a perfunctory fashion, or throw themselves into prayer only when they require the services of a Santa God? Yet if prayer is that activity in which we most self-consciously attempt to speak with and listen to God, then it should be the most important thing we Christians do. To complicate matters even more, we're called upon not merely to pray once in awhile, but to pray "everywhere,"[1] on "all occasions,"[2] and "unceasingly"[3]! Prayerful communion with God is not meant to be just another activity in a busy life; instead, it properly functions as a Christian's spiritual center of gravity. To become and continue as a person of prayer is the first duty of every Christian. That's why John Donne once exhorted in a sermon: "So whosoever you be, that cannot readily pray, at least pray that you may pray. For, as in bodily, so in spiritual diseases, it is a desperate state to be speechless."[4]

Why do we fall so short of the mark? Why do we

suffer from a spiritual malady that renders us speechless? For the most part, we fail to pray not because we're evil people, but because we simply don't know how to pray. We haven't been taught how to *do* prayer, nor how to integrate it into our lives so that we pray ceaselessly in the midst of our everyday activities. Of course, we've all memorized certain fixed, formulaic prayers. But glassy-eyed recitation is a Monty Pythonish caricature of genuine praying; rotely mouthing the words of a prayer is not the same thing as *doing* prayer. As Teresa of Avila warns, if a person "merely utters the words that come to his lips because he has learned them by heart through constant repetition, I do not call that prayer at all and God grant no Christian may ever speak to Him so!"[5] Likewise, of course, we've all dropped to our knees in desperation to cajole or bully God into pulling our chestnuts out of the fire. But as the movie *Priest* brings home, prayer must be more than a merely ad hoc expediency. Demanding that the divine cavalry rush to the rescue isn't prayer so much as insolence. But it's an insolence which, like rote recitation, usually springs more from ignorance about the true nature of prayer than from ill will.

The obvious failing in the Monty Python and *Priest* approaches to prayer is that God gets upstaged by meaningless phrases in the one case and self-centered desperation in the other. But true prayer, genuine prayer, ceaseless prayer, joyful prayer, is always focused squarely on God. Otherwise, what passes for prayer is nothing more than a symptom of the spiritual disease Donne cautions against. A legend about the Baal Shem Tov, Hasidism's founder, gets this point across beautifully:

> Once the Baal Shem stopped on the threshold of a House of Prayer and refused to go in. I cannot enter, he said. It is crowded with teaching and prayers

from wall to wall and from floor to ceiling. How could there be room for me? When he saw that those around him were staring, unable to understand, he added: The words of those whose teaching and praying does not come from the hearts lifted to heaven, cannot rise to heaven; instead, their words fill the house from wall to wall and from floor to ceiling.[6]

Our two retreat directors, Brother Lawrence and the Russian Pilgrim, are aware of the danger of cluttering up the heart's temple with leaden, lifeless prayers. For them, prayer is that interior movement which liberates us to soar to the sacred throne. When we pray authentically we are in the presence of God. Initially this is a frightful place in which to find ourselves. Who, after all, can stand before the living God and not be consumed? Who can see God and live? But gradually, as one grows into the prayerful life—or, more accurately, as the Holy Spirit leads one more deeply into it—the realization dawns that such immolation is precisely the point. The final purpose of prayer is to offer ourselves up as oblations to God, to be so consumed by the high intensity of divine Love that our petulant demands and self-pitying petitions and indifferent hearts melt away. When this happens, we are no longer persons who *say* prayers. We are persons who have *become* prayers. This is the mystery at which Saint Paul's injunction to "pray ceaselessly" gestures.

Luke tells us that Jesus' original disciples once sat around him and watched with wonderment as he prayed. After he finished, they beseeched him: "Lord, teach us to pray."[7] So say all followers of Christ. Every generation of disciples must be taught anew how to pray. Jesus, of course, is the first and primary teacher, but there are many adepts who, having sat at his feet, can likewise instruct us. Two of them direct this retreat. So, with humility and hope, let us say to Brother Lawrence and the Russian Pilgrim: "Teach us to pray."

Opening Prayer

Father in Heaven! Show unto us a little patience; for we often intend in all sincerity to commune with Thee and yet we speak in such a foolish fashion. Sometimes, when we judge that what has come to us is good, we do not have enough words to thank Thee; just as a mistaken child is thankful for having gotten his own way. Sometimes things go so badly that we call upon Thee; we even complain and cry unto Thee; just as an unreasoning child fears what would do him good. Oh, but if we are so childish, how far from being true children of Thine who art our true Father, ah, as if an animal would pretend to have man as a father. How childish we are and how little our proposals and our language resemble the language which we ought to use with Thee! We understand at least that it ought not to be thus and that we ought to be otherwise. Have then a little patience with us.[8]

RETREAT SESSION ONE

✟ Saint Teresa of Avila, that wonderfully feisty, independent and devout woman of God, prefaced one of her books on the practice of prayer with this pledge: "I shall speak of nothing of which I have no experience, either in my own life or in observation of others, or which the Lord has not taught me in prayer."[9] Her steadfast reliance on firsthand experience when it comes to prayer makes good sense. It's also the approach taken and taught by Brother Lawrence and the Russian Pilgrim.

We busy humans are generally content to get our information second- and third-hand from books, magazines, television or casual conversation. In most cases, this sort of pre-digested news is quite adequate. But there are certain insights which simply must be gathered firsthand. No one who wants to learn how to swim would go about it merely by reading interviews with Olympic champions. Similarly, we don't learn to love by listening to academic lectures on the psychology of love. We jump into water, albeit with some expert supervision, if we wish to swim, and we give ourselves to others, again (it is to be hoped) with good advice from mentors, if we wish to love. Immediate experience, not abstract theory, is essential in both cases.

The same can be said about prayer. It's wise and proper to seek counsel from spiritual directors when one wants to learn how to pray (otherwise retreats like this one would be quite beside the point!), or to consult theological and devotional books. But there's a great temptation to substitute the abstract study of prayer for the act of praying itself. It takes little effort to see that thinking about prayer is very much different from actually doing it. Chances are good, after all, that many of us on this retreat have read a number of books on prayer. Yet how many of us are satisfied with our prayer lives? No, mere abstract knowledge acquired second- and thirdhand is no more useful for learning to pray than for learning to swim or love. Hands-on experience, as the Russian Pilgrim learned, is what counts. Early in his spiritual journey he traveled from church to church, listening to countless sermons in the hope of learning how to pray. But the priests "always talked about getting ready for prayer, or about its fruits and the like, without teaching one *how* to pray." His conclusion was that the best way to discover answers to "primary and essential" questions such as "what is prayer?" and "how does one pray?", was simply to pray.[10] The Benedictine Dom John Chapman agrees. "The only way to pray," he advises, "is to pray, and the way to pray well is to pray much. If one has no time for this, then one must at least pray regularly. But the less one prays, the worse it goes."[11]

There are many reasons why even the best-intentioned of us settle for a bookish, abstract acquaintance with prayer, but the two most obvious ones are laziness and fear. Genuine prayer, prayer which comes from the heart and not merely the lips, is (at least initially) hard work. It requires concentration and discipline, and most of all it demands that we integrate our prayer life into the warp and woof of everyday existence rather than ghettoizing it to set-aside "devotional" times. Brother Lawrence worried that people too often content themselves with formalistic "petty acts of devotion" rather than integrating prayer into their daily routines. The Russian Pilgrim concurred: "We are lucky if we manage to say our ordinary prayers without slothfulness," he observed.[12] How much more difficult to pray from the heart and to pray ceaselessly!

But spiritual sloth is only part of the reason we prefer thinking and conversing about prayer to actually doing it. We fear putting our foot too deeply into the water of prayer because we sense irresistible undercurrents in its depths which are likely to carry us where we do not wish to go.[13] This anxiety was made especially clear to the Russian Pilgrim one day as he listened to a rather fatuous Polish steward discourse on prayer. "All that is necessary to fulfill one's duty to God," declared the steward, "is to pray simply, to stand and say the Our Father as Christ taught us. That puts you right for the whole day; but not to go on over and over again to the same tune." Up to this point the steward's casual attitude toward prayer seems to stem from old-fashioned laziness. But then the truth slips out. Praying constantly, the steward confides with a knowing air, "is, if I may say so, enough to drive you mad."[14]

"It's enough to drive you mad": The steward's wariness about the possible consequences of sustained prayer is shared by many of us, even though we may not be quite as blunt as he was. More typically, we put it like this: A person of prayer—that is, someone who puts prayerful communion with God before everything else— is a fanatic. A person of prayer is irrational. A person of prayer is too otherworldly and impractical. A person of prayer is visionary (meaning, of course, slightly cracked). Note that all these expressions imply that the person of prayer has somehow lost self-determination and autonomy. That's our real fear: that growing into prayer will change who we are and interfere with our carefully contrived plans and ambitions.

And there's good reason for the fear. Genuine prayer *does* take us out of ourselves by refocusing our attention away from the ego toward where it properly ought to be: God. Sometimes the observable consequences are dramatic. When deeply immersed in prayer, Brother Lawrence frequently capered like a joyful child and the Russian Pilgrim lost all awareness of his physical surroundings.[15] But the real transformation goes on beneath the surface. Giving oneself to prayer is a gradual letting-go of one's ego and a growing eagerness to follow the divine lead. The Polish steward saw this as madness. Saint Paul, for one, agreed, but qualified it as *divine* madness—a foolishness in and for Christ.[16]

But, of course, all this is easier said than done. Granted, praying is better than thinking about praying.

Granted again, laziness and fear hold us back from entering more fully into prayer. Granted, finally, that all the sermons and books and rituals in the world can't substitute for the actual doing of prayer. So how do we get started?

Sometimes we find it difficult to resolve questions because we search for overly complex solutions. This may be what goes on when we try to figure out how to pray. The BBC production of William Nicholson's *Shadowlands*, a drama about C. S. Lewis and Joy Davidman, clues us in to this. At one point in the film, Nicholson has the character Lewis say something about Christian faith which is perfectly applicable to prayer:

> I learned how to dive the same summer I learned I was a Christian. It's the easiest thing in the world. You don't have to *do* anything. All you have to do is stop doing something. You have to learn to *stop* trying to preserve yourself. Once you let yourself go headfirst without worrying where you're going to land or anything, it works. You're a diver!

How do we begin to pray? The first step, as Lewis says, is simply to jump in headfirst. The water is frightening—undertows, remember? But it does no good merely dabbing your toes in the shallows. Quit worrying about self-control—it's illusory for the most part anyway. Let go of your precious ego. Just let yourself slide into the water and trust that it will buoy you up. That, after all, is the kind of trustful abandonment symbolized by our going under into the waters of Baptism.

The spiritual life is one of profligacy. It demands such a generous spending of love and trust that the only possible outcome is bankruptcy—what Jesus in the Sermon on the Mount called "poverty [the word *ptōches* means "destitution"] of spirit." We become poor in spirit when we toss our tightly clutched egos to the wind and abandon ourselves to God. Likewise, we begin the journey toward ceaseless prayer of the heart when we abandon ourselves to the doing of praying, throwing ourselves unreservedly, profligately, into its uncharted waters. As Brother Lawrence advises, "we should give ourselves utterly to God in pure abandonment, in temporal and spiritual matters alike."[17] The early nineteenth-century missionary Francis Libermann likewise knew that once we quit battling the loss of self-control, once we cease resisting the Holy Spirit's invitation, we open ourselves up to the possibility of ceaseless prayer. "[P]lease, Lord," he wrote, "plunge me into your heavenly waters. Drown me in them; drown my passions, my pride, and all my vices and faults, that whatever in me comes from myself may die and the old creature be no more, and that there be nothing else in me than you."[18]

As we'll discover in tomorrow's retreat session, prayerful diving isn't as difficult as it may sound. Our nature as children of God predisposes us to it: We take to spiritual depths like ducks take to water. The problem is that we've forgotten what and who we are, and so the initial plunge is difficult. But as C. S. Lewis reminds us: The thing is just to dive!

For Reflection

- Henri Nouwen has this to say about prayer: "If we say that it's good to turn to God in prayer for a spare minute, or if we grant that a person with a problem does well to take refuge in prayer, we have as much as admitted that praying is on the margin of life and doesn't really matter."[19] Think about your current prayer life. Are you a marginal person of prayer? Can you see yourself as a member of Monty

*Python's listless congregation, or shrieking in desperate
fear with the young vicar in* Priest? *How might these
insights prompt you to take more care with your prayer
life?*

- *Do you find yourself thinking and reading about prayer
  more than actually praying? How do laziness and fear
  hamper your growth into prayer? What are other
  roadblocks in your prayer life?*

- *Recall the story told by Matthew (8:24-26) about Jesus and
  his disciples on the raging sea: "A windstorm arose on the
  sea, so great that the boat was being swamped by the
  waves; but [Jesus] was asleep And [the disciples] went and
  woke him up, saying, 'Lord, save us! We are perishing.'
  And he said to them, 'Why are you afraid, you of little
  faith?'"*

- *In what ways are you profligate in your spiritual life?*

Much of our backwardness in prayer is no doubt
due...to the very worst kind of "fear of God." We
shrink from too naked a contact, because we are
afraid of the divine demands upon us which it
might make too audible. As some old writer says,
many a Christian prays faintly "lest God might
really hear him, which he, poor man, never
intended."[20]

Closing Prayer

Jesus Christ, once your disciples came to you and
demanded: "Lord, teach us how to pray." You did as they
asked, and taught them the prayer whose holy words
have never left man's lips since then and which will rise
up from this day to the end of the world.

You gave this teaching for all men and forever; nothing will be removed from it, indeed, something yet will be added to it. But it helps only if you give it always anew, to each of us and at every hour. And so we also say: "Lord, teach us to pray."

Teach me to understand that without prayer my inner being languishes and my life loses balance and strength. Rid me of the talk about suffering and need, which serves to conceal laziness and rebellion. Give me seriousness and a firm purpose and help me to learn through conquering what is needed for salvation. Lead me also into your holy presence. Teach me to talk to you in the serious tones of truth and with the heartfelt accents of love.[21]

Notes

[1] 1 Timothy 2:8.

[2] Ephesians 6:18.

[3] 1 Thessalonians 5:17.

[4] John Donne, *Selections from Divine Poems, Sermons, Devotions, and Prayers*, John Booty, ed. (New York: Paulist Press, 1990), p. 189.

[5] *Interior Castle*, p. 32.

[6] *Gates of Prayer: The New Union Prayerbook* (New York: Central Conference of American Rabbis, 1975), p. 3.

[7] Luke 11:1.

[8] Perry D. LeFevre, ed., *The Prayers of Kierkegaard* (Chicago: University of Chicago Press, 1963), p. 19.

[9] Teresa of Avila, *The Way of Perfection*, E. Allison Peers, trans. (Garden City, N.Y.: Image, 1964), pp. 34-35.

[10] *Way of a Pilgrim*, pp. 7-8.

[11] Dom Roger Hudleston, ed., *The Spiritual Letters of Dom John Chapman* (London: Sheed and Ward, 1935), p. 53; quoted in Michael Casey, *Toward God: The Ancient Wisdom of Western Prayer* (Liguori, Mo.: Triumph, 1996), p. 50.

[12] *Practice of the Presence of God*, p. 20; *Way of a Pilgrim*, p. 75.

[13] I suspect this is what Jesus is hinting at when he tells Peter that as he grows in the spiritual life, "Someone else will fasten a belt

around you and take you where you do not wish to go" (John 21:18).

[14] *Way of a Pilgrim*, pp. 54-55.

[15] See, for example, *Practice of the Presence of God*, pp. 27, 35; *Way of a Pilgrim*, pp. 20-21, 39.

[16] 1 Corinthians 4:10.

[17] *Practice of the Presence of God*, p. 20.

[18] Anthony F. Chiffolo, ed., *At Prayer with the Saints* (Liguori, Mo.: Liguori, 1998), p. 124.

[19] Henri J. M. Nouwen, *With Open Hands*, Patrick Gaffney, trans. (New York: Ballantine, 1985), p. 50.

[20] C. S. Lewis, *Letters to Malcolm: Chiefly on Prayer* (New York: Harcourt Brace Jovanovich, 1964), pp. 113, 114.

[21] Romano Guardini, *Prayers from Theology*, Richard Newnham, trans. (New York: Herder & Herder, 1959), pp. 55-56.

DAY TWO
The Secret Prayer

Coming Together in the Spirit *hopeful*

Some commentators describe Psalm 42 as a biblical version of the somber "dark night of the soul" experience because they read it as the lament of a weary heart separated from God. But in fact it's a song of hopeful longing rather than despair. Although the psalmist feels downcast and forlorn, he also trusts that some day his spirit will be full enough again for him to praise God with glad hosannahs. This hope and yearning are expressed in the first lines of the psalm:

> As a deer longs for flowing streams,
> so my soul longs for you, O God.
> My soul thirsts for God,
> for the living God.
> When shall I come and behold
> the face of God?[1]

The early Church was particularly taken with this image of the soul as a thirsty creature yearning for the living waters of God. Psalm 42 was joyfully chanted at Easter when adult catechumens were baptized, and the font to which they were led was taken to represent the flowing spring of life to which their spiritual thirst had drawn them. Yearning, longing, burning desire—these are the signs of a soul struggling to make its way back to God, back to its divine source. They are disturbing, but also laden with promise and hope. They whisper to us that our thirst would not exist were there not sweet waters to quench it. These revivifying streams run deeply both in and around us. They are the groundwater of our souls. We sniff their aroma and ache with the sweetness of it. As Augustine reminds us in his *Confessions*, we are made for such waters, and our hearts are restless until we drink our fill of them.[2]

Defining Our Thematic Context

During the first day of our retreat, Brother Lawrence and the Russian Pilgrim helped us understand that we tend to avoid prayer either out of sloth or fear of losing self-control. But the only way to surmount these obstacles and enter into prayer is by praying—not thinking about prayer or reading about it, but actually *doing* it. This in turn demands that we abandon ourselves to the unplumbed depths of the divine ocean (we must dive, as Nicholson's C. S. Lewis says), and there's no getting around the fact that this is an intimidating prospect.

Today our retreat directors remind us that the leap into prayer is not simply frightening. It's also deeply fulfilling. It is frightening because it takes us out of our customary, comfortable places and onto sacred ground. All mortals quake before the burning bush. But it is fulfilling because our heart's deepest desire in fact *is* the burning bush, the numinous presence of God which consumes without destroying. This desire is always with us, even though many of us misunderstand its true object. Even when we are too confused or hardened to pray consciously or deliberately, the heart-longing deep within us reaches out towards the sacred that is both its source and destination. This desire, as the Russian Pilgrim says, is a secret prayer. It is a sign that at our most profound level we are naturally inclined to prayer.[3] The methodical practice of ceaseless prayer, then, is the effort to live deliberately what one already is by design.

Opening Prayer

Almighty and eternal god,
Thou art hidden from my sight:
Thou art beyond the understanding of my mind;
Thy thoughts are not my thoughts;
Thy ways are past finding out.

Yet hast Thou breathed Thy Spirit into my life:
Yet hast Thou formed my mind to seek Thee:
Yet hast Thou inclined my heart to love Thee:
Yet hast Thou made me restless for the rest that
    is in Thee:
Yet has Thou planted within me a hunger and
    thirst that
make me dissatisfied with all the joys of earth.[4]

Retreat Session Two

Aristotle believed that nature does nothing in vain. For every essential human desire, he taught, there must exist some object capable of assuaging it. We experience physical hunger and thirst, for example, and food and drink satisfy these desires. But we also appear to have a native longing for beauty and love and truth that goes every bit as deep as our appetite for bread or water. We feel within our hearts the ache for something which transcends the here-and-now, and no physical object seems capable of soothing it. We stand before a painting or listen to a piece of music and greedily drink in its beauty; we throw ourselves into romantic affairs in an effort to satisfy our longing for ultimate love; we devour books of philosophy to satisfy the yearning for truth. And yet, as the twentieth-century mystic Simone Weil observes, "We still desire something. We do not in the least know what it is.... It is a...mystery that is painfully tantalizing."[5]

But if Aristotle is correct, there must be something which satisfies our deepest longings. Brother Lawrence and the Russian Pilgrim think there is. The ultimate object of our heart's desire is the transcendent source of worldly beauty and love and truth. When we are drawn to a lovely piece of art, to human love, or to philosophical wisdom, it's because we vaguely sense—through a glass darkly, as it were—absolute beauty and love and truth shining forth in each of them. It is the absolute, the unconditioned, the eternal, which truly attracts us. The slightest hint of its presence causes us to catch our breath in bittersweet yearning.

Why this yearning in the first place? Why the hunger for the unconditioned? Because we have a natural affinity to it. Saint Augustine is correct: What we call the *super*natural is our *natural* element. God, the absolute, unconditioned, eternal God, made us for himself out of himself. We are flesh of his flesh, bone of his bone. God the absolute Parent, the unconditioned Mother, the eternal Father, is our origin, and our spiritual DNA resonates with a chthonic understanding of this truth. Like calls to like. The trace of God in us quivers with exhilarated recognition when it encounters traces of God in worldly displays of beauty, love and truth. Our souls are naturally

God-hungry; this is the mystery which tantalized Simone Weil. We are deer panting in the desert, forever stirred by dim memories of the cool waters which birthed us and gave us suckle.

But the God to whom we are unbreakably connected isn't just our source. He's also our end. Our destiny as creatures made in God's image is to live up to our potential by becoming Godlike: "You shall be holy, for I the LORD your God am holy."[6] This means that we increasingly attune to the Spirit within us until *its* will becomes *our* will. "O image of God," proclaimed William of St. Thierry, "recognize your dignity, allow the imprint of your Maker to shine out from you."[7] The Greek Fathers called this spiritual growth *theopoesis* or "deification." Saint Maximos the Confessor says it is a process in which the "participant become[s] like that in which he participates"—that is, grows increasingly like God. When this happens, God interpenetrates the human soul and the human soul interpenetrates God in an "ever-active repose."[8]

The contemporary thinker Ludwig Wittgenstein once remarked that true religion is a sigh because at the end of the day all our theology and liturgy is an expression of the heart's deep yearning for union with its divine source and destination.[9] This, of course, is the same intuition Saint Maximos expressed in his remarks on deification. The Russian Pilgrim goes one step farther by observing, as we've already noted, that the sigh of longing for God which is our essential nature is in fact a prayer, a "secret prayer"—*secret* because it "lies hidden within the human heart." We may not recognize it as such because we're accustomed to thinking of prayer as worded petitions or praises. But the "innate aspiration of every soul toward God," just like all of creation's mysterious sighing for the Creator (cf. Romans 8:18) "is exactly what interior prayer is."[10]

Some fifteen centuries earlier Saint Augustine expressed the same insight in one of his homilies. Puzzled by the scriptural injunction to pray ceaselessly, he concluded that although continuous conventional prayer is not possible, an unceasing longing for God—the Pilgrim's "secret prayer"—is.

> For it is thy heart's desire that is thy prayer; and if thy desire continues uninterrupted, thy prayer continueth also. For not without a meaning did the Apostle say, "Pray without ceasing." Are we to be "without ceasing" bending the knee, prostrating the body, or lifting up our hands, that he says, "Pray without ceasing"? Or if it is in this sense that we say we "pray," this, I believe, we cannot do "without ceasing." There is another inward kind of prayer without ceasing, which is the desire of the heart. Whatever else you are doing, if you do but long for that Sabbath, you do not cease to pray. If you would never cease to pray, never cease to long after it. The continuance of thy longing is the continuance of thy prayer.[11]

Elsewhere Augustine puts the matter in its simplest form: "When does prayer sleep? When desire has grown cold."[12]

If our native longing for reunion with the divine source is itself a secret prayer, the obvious conclusion to be drawn is that we already pray, constantly, with every heartbeat. The Russian Pilgrim acknowledges as much when he says that "there is no need to learn [prayer], it is innate in every one of us."[13] But if this is true, why do many of us feel so out of touch with prayer?

The answer is that we've forgotten what our restless longing signifies. This is another reason why the Pilgrim calls it a "secret" prayer. We are born with an innate knowledge of what will ultimately satisfy us, but we

allow ourselves to be so distracted as the years roll by
that it gets buried. So we interpret our restlessness as
desire for possessions, for sexual gratification, for public
recognition, for power—as anything, in short, except
what it is—and frantically pursue these will-o'-the-wisps
with varying degrees of success. But a hunger for the
Absolute can never be satisfied by such paltry fare. The
more money and objects and prestige we acquire, the
more restless we grow. Our ill-conceived diet slowly
starves us to death.

To make matters worse, we can slip into a spiritual
inertia that settles for the commonplace objects with
which we try to feed our hunger. We forget the profound
significance of our sigh of longing, forget that it's directed
at both God and our own selves as images of God. When
this happens, the Pilgrim says, "we live far from
ourselves and have but little wish to get any nearer to
ourselves." Brother Lawrence agrees; spiritual inertia
prevents us from seeing God "in the depths of our soul."
Both men lament that we settle instead for "trifles."[14]

The only way to liberate ourselves from the deadly
spiral caused by our confused restlessness is to recollect
the truth about our innate hunger for God. The Greek
word for "truth" is *aletheia*. It's the word the Gospel of
John uses, for example, when describing Jesus (John 14:6)
as the way, the "truth," and the life. *Aletheia* has several
meanings, but one of the most insightful is "unforgetting."
We are in the truth when we recall or unforget what we
once knew but have allowed to slip out of our awareness.

In the context of prayer, we are in the truth when we
unforget the secret prayer that lies at the core of who we
are. We unforget that the yearning within us is for the
absolute, unconditioned and eternal source from which
we came. As the Pilgrim puts it, such unforgetting
"arouse[s] in your soul a thirst and a longing...which

brings you an insatiable desire to know things more closely and more fully, to go deeper into their nature."[15] We unforget that we, like the prodigal son, are forever united with the divine Parent, regardless of how far we stray. In Brother Lawrence's words, "God is present before you whatever you are doing…, he is at the depth and centre of your soul."[16] Finally, we unforget that this everlasting intimacy is a cause for joy and celebration— for a bedazzled and sweet "bliss," as the Russian Pilgrim says.[17]

But how to unforget all this? Brother Lawrence and the Pilgrim agree that there are two necessary conditions. The first is the illuminating presence of God within our souls—or, in other words, grace. The second is a steadfast cooperation on our part with divine grace.

The first condition for unforgetting is always and everywhere fulfilled. Thomas Merton reminds us that God is "the Life Who dwells and sings within the essence of every creature and in the core of our souls."[18] A century before Merton, Theophan the Recluse had the same intuition. "You seek the Lord?" he asked. "Seek, but only within yourself…. Everyone who meets the Lord meets Him there. He has fixed no other place for meeting souls."[19] As we've already noted, we come from God, and our spiritual genetic code carries unerasable traces of that divine lineage. We are temples of the Holy, if we but knew it. The secret prayer of longing throbs in the human heart because God dwells in the human heart. In diving inwards toward prayer we land in the arms of Christ.

Brother Lawrence knew this. When we pray, he says, "It is only necessary to realise that God is intimately present within us." Similarly, the Pilgrim insists that prayer is not possible until we realize that "the kingdom of God is revealed in our hearts."[20] This realization of God's presence is initiated by grace. "The man himself does not know it, yet working mysteriously within his soul [the Holy Spirit] urges him to prayer according to each man's knowledge and power." And again, "It is prayer itself"—the indwelling nudge of God—"which will reveal to you how it can be achieved unceasingly."[21]

The second condition for unforgetting the secret prayer is up to us. God lays the foundation, but we are the co-builders. We must deliberately attune ourselves to the secret prayer unceasingly murmured by the Holy Spirit and purposefully allow it to surface to consciousness. Such attunement calls for a spiritual discipline. The one practiced by our two retreat directors consists of three teachings: (1) an awareness of the distractions that block our unforgetting of the secret prayer; (2) the necessity of deafening ourselves to those distractions long enough to listen to the secret prayer; and (3) a technique for so embracing the secret prayer that we and it become one, or "interpenetrate" one another. These steps are the foci, respectively, of our next three retreat sessions.

Unforgetting the secret prayer calls, then, for active collaboration on our part, and the spiritual discipline taught by Brother Lawrence and the Russian Pilgrim tutors us in the dynamics of that collaboration. We saw earlier that our spiritual inertia often prompts us to grab the easy out of fixating on immediate objects of desire instead of the living water for which we truly pant. The same inertia can also seduce us into presuming that to make contact with the secret prayer all we need do is sit back and let God do the work.

But this is a falsehood. The secret prayer, the indwelling Spirit, continuously calls to us, offering us kairetic opportunities for spiritual transformation. But such opportunities are lost unless we shake off our sloth, timidity or complacency long enough to get up and take advantage of them. Saint Paul famously received his opportunity on the road to Damascus. Brother Lawrence encountered his in that winter-blasted garden and the Russian Pilgrim as he listened to Scripture. But none of these men would have achieved a state of unforgetfulness had they not actively embraced the *kairos*-gift offered them and then labored for the rest of their lives to understand and grow into it. This kind of labor calls for resolute discipline. The Pilgrim reminds us that even though deification, or "perfection" as he calls it, ultimately is a gift from God, we are still called to cooperate with the work of the Holy Spirit. The road will be long and hard. Our growth may even seem imperceptible for years on end. But the main thing is "to pray often, to pray always." This, at least, "falls within our power."[22]

The poet Denise Levertov hauntingly echoes the Pilgrim's claim that engaged perseverance is required for growing into the God who prays within us. In her poem "Conversion of Brother Lawrence," she retells the story of the wind-stripped tree, "[w]ooden lace, a celestial geometry," which for Lawrence was a "twig-winged angel of annunciation" proclaiming God's invitation. But Levertov doesn't stop there. She knows that receiving the invitation is one thing, responding in steadfast and disciplined faithfulness another. What distinguished Brother Lawrence from so many others who have also heard the kairetic call is that, in spite of everything, he persevered to the end.

Out from the chateau park it sent you
(by some back lane, no doubt,
not through the wide gates of curled iron),
by ways untold, by soldier's marches, to the
    obscure
clatter and heat of a monastery kitchen,
a broom's rhythmic whisper for music,
your torment the drudgery of household ledgers.
    Destiny
without visible glory. 'Time pressed.' Among pots
    and pans,
heart-still through the bustle of chores,
your labors, hard as the pain in your lame leg,
grew slowly easier over the years, the years
when, though your soul felt darkened, heavy,
    worthless,
yet God, you discovered, never abandoned you
    but walked
at your side keeping pace as comrades had
on the long hard roads of war. You entered then
the unending 'silent secret conversation,'
the life of steadfast attention.[23]

Thus did Brother Lawrence cooperate with God to uncover the secret prayer, that deep well of living water for which his soul thirsted. And so must we.

For Reflection

■ *Reread the story of the encounter between Jesus and the woman at the well (John 4:7-30). Meditate on the words spoken by Jesus: "Everyone who drinks of [worldly] water will be thirsty again, but those who drink of the water that I will give them will never be thirsty. The water that I give will become in them a spring of water gushing up to eternal life."*

- *When have you experienced moments of intense longing for the unconditioned that were triggered by encounters with beauty, love or truth? How did the experience point beyond itself to its divine source?*

- *What are some of the "junk foods" you habitually gorge on to satisfy your restless longing for union with God? How does spiritual inertia reveal itself in other ways in your life?*

- *Reflect on the claim that the Spirit of God is within you, and that its nudging constitutes a secret prayer. In what ways do you actively cooperate with the divine nudging? When have you sat back and expected God to lead you by the nose?*

- *Saint Maximos the Confessor says that our final destiny is to achieve such an intimate "interpenetration" with the God within that we forever repose actively in him. How do you envision this "active repose"? Does the prospect of such an active repose fill you with longing or fright? With both? Why?*

- *Recall the moment you first heard God's invitation. Are you satisfied with the steadfastness of your response to it?*

On the second day of Creation, God separated the upper and lower waters. At the moment of their separation, we are told, the lower waters cried out: "We too long to be near our Creator!"

So it is with the soul: it too once dwelt in the upper realms, near to God, and has fallen to the lowest depths. Like the lower waters of Creation, it cries out to return to God. "Pour out your heart like the waters," says the Psalmist, longing again to be "in the Presence of the Lord."[24]

Closing Prayer

Lord Jesus Christ, pierce my soul with thy love so that I may always long for thee alone, who art the bread of angels and the fulfillment of the soul's deepest desires. May my heart always hunger and feed upon thee, so that my soul may be filled with the sweetness of thy presence. May my soul thirst for thee, who art the source of life, wisdom, knowledge, light and all the riches of God our Father. May I always seek and find thee, think upon thee and do all things for the honour and glory of thy name. Be always my only hope, my peace, my refuge and my help in whom my heart is rooted so that I may never be separated from thee.[25]

Notes

[1] Psalm 42:1 2.

[2] "You have made us for yourself, and our heart is restless until it rests in you." Augustine, *Confessions*, Henry Chadwick, trans. (Oxford: Oxford University Press, 1992), p. 3.

[3] *Way of a Pilgrim*, p. 189.

[4] John Baillie, *A Diary of Private Prayer* (New York: Scribners, 1949), p. 21.

[5] Simone Weil, *Waiting for God*, Emma Craufurd, trans. (New York: Putnam's, 1951), p. 166.

[6] Leviticus 19:2.

[7] William of St. Thierry, *On the Song of Songs*, 66; quoted in *Toward God*, p. 29.

[8] St. Maximos the Confessor, "Various Texts on Theology, the Divine Economy, and Virtue and Vice," in *The Philokalia*, G.E.H. Palmer, Philip Sherrard, Kallistos Ware, eds. and trans. (London: Faber & Faber, 1981), vol. 2, p. 239.

[9] Antony Kenny, ed., *A Wittgenstein Reader* (Oxford: Basil Blackwell, 1995), p. 298.

[10] *Way of a Pilgrim*, pp. 63, 43.

[11] Augustine, "Homily on Psalm 38," in *Expositions on the Book of*

Psalms, A. Cleveland Coxe, trans., in *Nicene and Post-Nicene Fathers* (Peabody, Mass.: Hendrickson, 1994), p. 107.

[12] Augustine, "Sermon 80"; quoted in Boniface Ramsey, *Beginning to Read the Fathers* (Mahwah, N.J.: Paulist Press, 1985), pp. 171-172.

[13] *Way of a Pilgrim*, p. 43.

[14] *Way of a Pilgrim*, p. 79; *Practice of the Presence of God*, p. 83.

[15] *Way of a Pilgrim*, pp. 131-32.

[16] *Practice of the Presence of God*, p. 69.

[17] *Way of a Pilgrim*, p. 38.

[18] Thomas Merton, *Seeds of Contemplation*, p. 16.

[19] *The Art of Prayer*, p. 187.

[20] *Practice of the Presence of God*, p. 28; *Way of a Pilgrim*, p. 81.

[21] *Ibid.*, pp. 63, 4.

[22] *Ibid.*, p. 9.

[23] Denise Levertov, "Conversion of Brother Lawrence," in *The Stream and the Sapphire* (New York: New Directions, 1997), p. 46.

[24] Hit'orerut Ha-Teffilah, quoted in Arthur Green and Barry W. Holtz, eds., *Your Word Is Fire: The Hasidic Masters on Contemplative Prayer* (Woodstock, Vt.: Jewish Lights, 1993), p. 78.

[25] *The Complete Book of Christian Prayer* (New York: Continuum, 1998), p. 4.

Day Three
Welcome to the Monkey House

Coming Together in the Spirit

The great hermit Saint Antony (251-356) took himself to the desert in search of the heart's secret prayer. But as his biographer Saint Athanasius famously recounts in the *Vita Antonii*, Antony discovered that diving is one thing and reaching bottom another. Antony had no problem taking the plunge. It's just that once in the water, he bumped up against unexpected hindrances.

Using the idiom of his day, Athanasius described these impediments as demons maliciously bent on tempting human souls away from prayerful encounters with the indwelling Spirit. Today we have a different idiom, and (for better or worse) think of the "demons" which plagued poor Antony as all those irrelevant ideas, desires, memories and fantasies which predictably flood and distract the mind of a person trying to pray. But whether we speak the language of demonology or psychology, the point is the same. Once we at last jump into the waters of prayer, we frequently find ourselves attacked by monsters of the deep whose purpose is to frighten or seduce us away from the single-minded search for God.

Saint Antony's desert temptations were a favorite

subject of medieval and Renaissance painters. Scores of canvases have come down to us which portray Antony in locked combat with a grotesque host of simian-like imps hell-bent on giving him a bad case of the spiritual bends. One of these paintings is by the sixteenth-century Matthias Grünewald, and it's truly nightmarish. A diabolical assault has thrown Antony on his back and the demons are closing in. One of them clutches Antony's hair, jerking him in one direction. Another has latched onto his right hand, tugging him in the opposite direction. The rest of the misshapen, hideous imps move in for the kill, sharpened sticks and razor-sharp talons hoisted to rip Antony to shreds. The situation seems utterly hopeless.[1]

Grünewald's bleak depiction of Antony's temptations is typical. Painters intrigued by the saint's desert struggle have focused mainly on its horror and black despair. This is understandable; all of us can relate to the spiritual chaos Antony must have felt as he reeled from the demonic attack. Who among us doesn't have firsthand experience of being so pulled in a thousand different directions during prayer that it feels as if the soul is being drawn and quartered? Even Jesus was harried by the demons of restlessness during his forty-day retreat in the wilderness.[2]

The imps of distraction are a fact of spiritual life. They stand between us and the secret prayer, jealously guarding its portals. When we dive we can expect to run up against them. This is what Jesus as well as Antony and thousands of other saints discovered in their own prayer journeys. There's no way to avoid the imps, and when they attack—we might as well be honest here—they do so ferociously. This is the sorry state of affairs confronting all of us who would enter ceaseless prayer, and it's senseless to whitewash it. To be forewarned is to be prepared.

Read again

Defining Our Thematic Content

We discovered yesterday that the dive into the waters of prayer, despite its initial scariness, is a movement to which our souls are predisposed and for which our hearts yearn. We are predisposed to it because we already carry within us a secret prayer, unceasingly murmured by the indwelling Holy Spirit, which forever beckons even to those of us who have forgotten it. We yearn for it because we sense, howsoever dimly, that deep diving is the way to discover the living water for which we pant.

We saw that the secret prayer is that grace-gift by which God offers himself to us and calls us toward eventual union. But our two spiritual directors also pointed out that the divine invitation must be accepted in the spirit of collaboration. God extends his hand and we must reach out to grasp it. This calls for steadfast resolve: first, to become aware of (or unforget) the hindrances to ceaseless prayer; second, to school ourselves in a spiritual technique capable of overcoming them. Days Four and Five of our retreat will focus on the latter. Today, Brother Lawrence and the Russian Pilgrim help us out on the former.

We'll discover, as Antony did so many centuries ago, that the primary obstacles to ceaseless prayer are those imps of distraction that pull us hither and yon, enticing us to pursue them instead of single-mindedly heading toward God. Sometimes they hit us over the head in a ham-fisted manner with what the Russian Pilgrim calls "vain thoughts and sinful ideas." But the imps are also extraordinarily clever at disguising themselves. Frequently they succeed in convincing us that they're angelic rather than demonic, and before we realize what's going on they've led us far into a wasteland of rock and shadow. Whether they bludgeon or seduce us, however, their aim is always the same: to deflect us from entering into the secret prayer.

The demons are strong and determined. They'll fight us to the last breath. There's good reason for this: Our embrace of the secret prayer sounds their death knell. When they battle against our purification, they're struggling for their lives. And why is our success their defeat? Because the demons of distraction which assail us are our own creations, the wreckage with which we foolishly clutter up our spiritual environment. They are born from the false self, that pitiful ego which takes its own will as the center of reality. The false self is increasingly imperiled as we move closer to the secret prayer, because the secret prayer forever whispered in our hearts by God is in fact our true self, our Christ-self. The false self knows that it must diminish as the Christ-self increases, and it calls forth the imps of distraction to derail the progress.

When Matthias Grünewald's Saint Antony fell beneath the demonic onslaught, he succumbed to the imperious demands of his false self. When we take the plunge into prayer, we risk falling under the knives and talons of our false selves. We would be foolish to take the danger lightly. When you think about it, the demons spawned by our egos and self-will are a lot more threatening than anything Hell could throw at us. ✝

Opening Prayer

Lord, not you,
it is I who am absent.
At first
belief was a joy I kept in secret,
stealing alone
into sacred places:
a quick glance, and away—and back,
circling.
I have long since uttered your name
but now
I elude your presence.
I stop
to think about you, and my mind
at once
like a minnow darts away,
darts
into the shadows, into gleams that fret
unceasing over
the river's purling and passing.
Not for one second
will my self hold still, but wanders
anywhere,
everywhere it can turn. Not you,
it is I am absent.
You are the stream, the fish, the light,
the pulsing shadow,
you the unchanging presence, in whom all
moves and changes.
How can I focus my flickering, perceive
at the fountain's heart
the sapphire I know is there?[3]

RETREAT SESSION THREE

The novelist Anthony Burgess tells an unsettling story about a young British civil servant stationed in Singapore at the turn of the century. It seems that every morning on his way to work the man strolled through the city's Botanical Garden, which was filled with free-roaming monkeys. He got into the habit of bringing along a loaf of bread and throwing bits of it to the prancing, hooting simians. Each morning more of them showed up and swarmed around the civil servant to demand their share of breakfast. But one day, either because he forgot or because he decided that enough was enough, the young man failed to bring the monkeys the repast they'd come to expect. At first surprised and then enraged by this neglect, the whole army of ravenous monkeys fell on him and literally tore him to pieces.[4]

Most immediately, Burgess's macabre little tale is an allegory about colonialism: The European *tuan* patronizingly throwing crumbs to natives whose lands he's invaded ought not to expect gratitude or loyalty from them. But the story conveys a great spiritual truth as well: Each of us is the young civil servant, and the host of monkeys shrieking at us is that chaotic jumble of ideas, desires, passions, memories and fears which clamor for our attention when we try to pray. The more we heed the monkeys' din and pause to feed them, the more they demand. If we don't put an end to this cycle, we soon find ourselves their captive. Then, if we risk pulling away, they try to tear us apart.

In the Buddhist tradition, this state of spiritual bondage is sometimes called "monkey mind." It's well named. We suffer from monkey mind when our spirits are so distracted by a jungle-full of confused thoughts and desires and worldly concerns that we're unable to focus prayerfully on God. We discover, as Saint Antony did, that the monkeys waiting to tug us in a thousand different directions are legion. When we throw bread at one of them, ten more take its place. Before we scarcely know what's happening, we're submerged in their cacophonous din.

Both of our spiritual directors forewarn us about monkey mind. The "mind is always given to roaving," cautions Brother Lawrence, and unless it's "early subdued," the "bad habits of wandering and inattention" which come to infect our prayer life will be "difficult to overcome."[5] When this happens, single-minded concentration "lamentably" succumbs to restless "human preoccupations."[6] The hesychast Theophan the Recluse, himself an admirer of the Russian Pilgrim's writings, concurred. "The chief enemy of life in God," he declared, "is a profusion of worldly cares." They hurl us into "an endless round" of activities, "from morning till night [driving us] from one job to another, [leaving us] no time to turn to God."[7]

If we would learn to pray unceasingly, then, we must quell our inner monkeys. And to do that, we first need to know how to recognize them when they appear.

So what do the monkey-imps look like? The ones easiest to spot are those random associations, memories and desires that seemingly crop up out of nowhere when we pray. We settle ourselves on a pew or kneeler, take a couple of deep breaths and try to calm our minds so that we may be receptive to God's spirit. But almost immediately the empty interior space we want to achieve overloads with irrelevant (and irreverent!) snatches of past conversations, future-oriented daydreams, workday schedules, sexual fantasies and reawakened grudges, all of which buzz around inside us with dizzying speed.

They tumble one on top of another, each giving rise to a multitude of free-wheeling associations, until we're over our heads in the roaring white water of consciousness. Despite our best intentions, we've dragged the noisy world of shopping lists, bills, gossip, headlines, feuds, advertising jingles, chores and infatuations into our prayer.

It's as if a film spliced together from thousands of disjointed frames is rolling nonstop in our heads. Or perhaps a better comparison is channel-surfing: It's as if we're flicking through channel after channel of mental television, not pausing long enough to catch much more than a scene here, a sound bite there. Like everything on television, the images by and large are stupidly pointless, but they're also horribly addictive. They require no effort on our part. They invite us simply to sit back and passively observe.

These kinds of monkeys are easy to spot. We immediately recognize them for the distractions they are. While this doesn't necessarily mean that we'll actually turn the mental television off, it at least shows that we feel guilty about wasting so much time in front of it when we ought to be concentrating on prayer. But there are other monkeys more difficult to see through. This is because they disguise their disruptive gibbering in the respectably well-modulated tones of theology, churchly aesthetics or comfortingly predictable acts of piety. We saw at the beginning of our retreat that many of us tend to substitute facsimiles of prayer for the genuine article. The more clever monkey-imps use this weakness for their own purposes. It's a terribly effective strategy, because it allows us to avoid prayer without guilt. It leaves no messy side effects of uneasy conscience.

Take theology. There is, of course, a place for it in the life of the Christian. We are called to think through the *ask I.P.*

articles of our faith with humility and rigor. But abstract theological thinking is inappropriate in prayer. We ought to theologize in a prayerful manner, and our theology ought to follow from our prayer lives. But prayer is not theological speculation, and when we confuse the two, we are distracted from the true nature and purpose of prayer.

Both Brother Lawrence and the Russian Pilgrim are grimly aware of the monkey of theological speculation. When it comes to praying, warns Lawrence, "thoughts spoil everything. All evil begins there. We must take care to set them aside as soon as we observe them not to be necessary for the task of the moment or for our salvation, so that we can begin again our converse with God, wherein is our only good."[8] The Russian Pilgrim agrees: "The mind and the heart are not one and the same thing."[9] Theology is a second-order child of the intellect, but genuine prayer arises immediately and spontaneously from the heart. The abstractions of theology, with their endless rounds of words and syllogisms and theories, are barriers between us and the pure experience of the secret prayer. "Reasonings...based upon speculation and the working of natural wisdom" substitute ideas for the "active experience" of prayer.[10] At best, Brother Lawrence cautions, they are "preliminaries."[11] We err when we mistake them for ends,[12] because in doing so we commune not with *God* but with our *ideas about* God. Thus what we take to be a single-minded focus on the Divine is actually a single-minded focus on our own intellectual chattering. We settle for "a bad copy" and "neglect" the "excellent original."[13]

Equally distracting and just as hard to recognize are the monkeys of spiritual beauty. Too often would-be persons of prayer mistake a concentration on eloquently poetic "religious" experiences for a prayerful focus on

God. The Russian Pilgrim tells us that beginners are especially susceptible to such "aesthetic" distractions, and he speaks from experience.

> My starets of blessed memory used to say that the forces which are against prayer in the heart attack us from two sides, from the left hand and from the right. That is to say, if the enemy cannot turn us from prayer by means of vain thoughts and sinful ideas, then he brings back into our minds good things we have been taught, and fills us with beautiful ideas, so that one way or another he may lure us away from prayer, which is a thing he cannot bear. It is called a "theft from the right-hand side," and in it the soul, putting aside its converse with God, turns to the satisfaction of converse with self or with created things. He taught me, therefore, not to admit during times of prayer even the most lofty of spiritual thoughts.[14]

Obviously, the Pilgrim's point isn't that spiritual beauty has no place in the Christian life. The soul is frequently moved in quite profound ways by the rich hues of a stained glass window, the sheer poetry of a sung mass, or the attractive and sometimes exhilarating style of a spiritual writer. As Dionysius the Areopagite noted, one of God's divine names is Beauty, and whenever we encounter beauty in the world we are irresistibly drawn towards the Beauty of God.[15] But just as theological speculation is not prayer, neither, says the Pilgrim, is "the mere enjoyment of spiritual things."[16] Pleasing experiences of beauty may lead us to prayer, but are not prayer in themselves. When mistaken for prayer, they are every bit as distracting as the monkeys of "vain thoughts and sinful ideas." As the Pilgrim says, they fixate on the self's delight in created things rather than leading us towards the supreme Creator.

Authentic prayer is also deflected by addiction to mechanical piety. Both Brother Lawrence and the Russian Pilgrim agree that short formulaic prayers as well as stylized ritual can help to quell the hubbub of the monkey house long enough for us to concentrate on God. But we cross over the line when worded prayer, along with conventional ritualized acts such as genuflections, candle-lighting, stations of the cross and so on, become means rather than ends. As Buddhists say, they are fingers pointing at the moon, not the moon itself, and if we fall into the trap of viewing them as anything more than pointers or "preliminaries" they become distractions. "Do not fetter yourself by rules or special forms of worship," cautions Brother Lawrence. "Petty acts of devotion" which gratify our sense of obligation should not become "our rule for living." Otherwise, we desert the secret prayer "for trifles."[17]

The monkeys which Lawrence calls petty acts of devotion deflect us from genuine prayer in two ways. First, they can become so comfortably routine that we perform them absentmindedly. On the surface, our fingers move from one rosary bead to the next and our lips rotely reel off the decades. But underneath, where it really counts, our minds are incessantly chattering away, busily preoccupied with anything and everything except the task at hand. Second, a mechanically scrupulous observance of ritualisms risks focusing our attention on ourselves rather than God. We begin to observe ourselves making the Sign of the Cross, kneeling or walking to the altar rail with properly pious expression, and before long we're too busy enjoying our own performance to pray. Like the Pharisees of Jesus' day, we entertain ourselves with outward displays of sanctimony, aiming, as a priest friend of mine observes, for "preciousness" rather than prayer.

There are, then, many residents in the monkey house of our mind, and all of them distract us from the focus necessary for genuine prayer. Some of these monkeys are boldly unembarrassed imps of the "left side" who seek to turn us away from God with "vain thoughts and sinful ideas." Others are more subtle succubi who attack from the "right side" by seducing us with theological abstractions, spiritual beauty, or conventional piety. What they all have in common is their loyalty to the false self, the demanding ego, the imperious "me," which fears and hates the rival Christ-self embedded within the secret prayer.

When the false self attacks with its "left" flank, we experience a head-on assault and face the danger of being overrun by regiments of irrelevant thoughts and desires. When the false self sends in the "right" flank, we're infiltrated by saboteurs who cunningly persuade us that we're focused on God when in fact we're not. Assailed from without or undermined from within: the false self fights the war on two fronts to scatter our attention and tear us away from the secret prayer. Before long, we're as trapped by our own monkeys as Anthony Burgess's civil servant was by his.

Moving toward the truth, as we saw yesterday, is a process of unforgetting. The first step in unforgetting is to recognize the monkeys of our false self for what they are. The second step is to resist them. That's the subject of Day Four's retreat.

For Reflection

- *Close your eyes, take a few deep breaths, and try to clear your mind. Are you able to do it, or is your inner world suddenly flooded with ideas, memories, images, sensations,*

fantasies, terrors and so on? Sit back and watch these
monkeys for a while; observe where and how far they take
you.

- *When you think about all the possible "vain thoughts and*
  sinful ideas"—the monkeys of the "left side"—that
  typically assault and scatter concentration, which ones are
  especially troublesome for you?

- *When your mental monkeys begin screeching for attention,*
  what kind of bread do you throw them? Do you resent
  feeding them, or do you rather enjoy it?

- *When do you find yourself succumbing to the monkeys of*
  the "right side"? In what ways? Theological speculation?
  Spiritual aestheticism? Pharisaic preciousness?

- *The thirteenth-century mystic Meister Eckhart once*
  remarked that it might be necessary to "throw away" God
  in order to "discover" God. Does Eckhart's observation
  shed any light for you on the monkeys of the "right side"?

- *Which of your qualities, habits and dispositions would you*
  say spring from the false self rather than the true Christ-
  self? Put a slightly different way, what would a profile of
  your false self look like?

God help my thoughts! They stray from me, setting
off on the wildest journeys; when I am at prayer,
they run off like naughty children, making trouble.
When I read the Bible, they fly to a distant place,
filled with seductions. My thoughts can cross an
ocean with a single leap; they can fly from earth to
heaven, and back again, in a single second. They
come to me for a fleeting moment, and then away
they flee. No chains, no locks can hold them back;
no threats of punishment can restrain them, no hiss
of a lash can frighten them. They slip from my grasp
like tails of eels; they swoop hither and thither like

swallows in flight.

Dear, chaste Christ, who can see into every heart,
and read every mind, take hold of my thoughts.
Bring my thoughts back to me, and clasp me to
yourself.[18]

Closing Prayer

O Lord, calm the waves of this heart; calm its
tempests! Calm thyself, O my soul, so that the divine can
act in thee! Calm thyself, O my soul, so that God is able to
repose in thee, so that His peace may cover thee! Yes,
Father in Heaven, often have we found that the world
cannot give us peace, O but make us feel that Thou art
able to give peace; let us know the truth of Thy promise:
that the whole world may not be able to take away Thy
peace.[19]

Notes

[1] Grünewald's Saint Antony is in the Museum Underlinden, Colmar.

[2] Matthew 4:1-11; Mark 1:12-13; Luke 4:1-13.

[3] Denise Levertov, "Flickering Mind," in *The Stream and the Sapphire*, pp. 15-16.

[4] Anthony Burgess, *Earthly Powers* (New York: Simon and Schuster, 1980), pp. 211-212.

[5] *Practice of the Presence of God*, p. 49.

[6] *Practice of the Presence of God*, p. 29.

[7] *The Art of Prayer*, p. 234.

[8] *Practice of the Presence of God*, p. 24.

[9] *Way of a Pilgrim*, p. 28.

[10] *Way of a Pilgrim*, p. 7.

[11] *Practice of the Presence of God*, p. 24.

[12] *Practice of the Presence of God*, p. 29.

[13] *Practice of the Presence of God*, p. 82.

[14] *Way of a Pilgrim*, pp. 67-68.

[15] Pseudo-Dionysius the Areopagite, *The Divine Names and Mystical Theology*, John D. Jones, trans. (Milwaukee: Marquette University Press, 1980), pp. 138-41.

[16] *Way of a Pilgrim*, p. 22.

[17] *Practice of the Presence of God*, pp. 42, 20, 83.

[18] A Celtic prayer of unknown source, in *The Complete Book of Christian Prayer*, p. 266.

[19] *Prayers of Kierkegaard*, p. 43.

Day Four
Heart-listening

Coming Together in the Spirit

Yesterday we reflected on Matthias Grünewald's painting of Saint Antony's struggle with the imps of distraction. Antony, you recall, has been knocked to the ground, and the demons are advancing to tear him to pieces and scatter him to the four winds. The painting is a visual parable about the ravaging effects of monkey mind.

But there's another side to Saint Antony's struggle which we who wish to pray ought never to forget. While it's true that the great desert father knew moments of despair and defeat when he tried to pray, it's also the case that he finally broke through all impediments to glide into the crystal clear waters of deep prayer.

A century before Grünewald, the Flemish painter Hieronymus Bosch wonderfully captured this spiritual triumph.[1] Bosch's Saint Antony sits by a riverside, his body relaxed, his face and eyes attentive without being taut. The grotesque imps who so tormented Grünewald's Antony are still present, but their power is broken. They can't touch Antony; he's aware of their presence, but unperturbed by it. Now it's the demons who experience frustrated defeat. One of them pops its head out of the river and leers at Antony in a futile attempt to distract him. Another, at wit's end, tries to disrupt the saint's

71

equilibrium by upturning a pot of soup on him. A third, apparently conceding that Antony is beyond his reach, peevishly consoles himself by clouting a nearby animal over the head. But Antony remains unflappable. The imps can chatter and prance and pull out every trick they have, but they'll never touch him. He's dived and broken through to the other side, and is hearkening so intently to what he's found there that he's oblivious to everything else. Antony has discovered the secret prayer, the indwelling Spirit of God. His false self has given way to the Christ-self.

This is the Saint Antony to keep in mind as we struggle with our own restlessness. Like us, he was distracted by the demons of desire and thought. But by God's grace, he persevered. He experienced firsthand what Scripture promises: The person who asks in good faith for spiritual food will not be handed a cold stone.[2]

Defining Our Thematic Context

When we were kids, many of us fell for a gag toy popularly called "Chinese handcuffs." A Chinese handcuff is an elastic cloth tube about three inches long. The trick is to get someone to stick his or her index fingers into either end of the snug tube and then try to yank them out. At first glance—and this is the grabber—it seems like the easiest thing in the world to do. But because the tube is elastic, it tightens up when the handcuffed person struggles to pull out of it. The harder he or she tugs to free the caught fingers, the more the tube clamps onto them.

The secret to getting out of Chinese handcuffs, of course, is not to struggle. Instead, what's necessary is to so relax the fingers that the tube just naturally falls right off them. But few of us have the patience or foresight to do that; we pull and strain and twist and yank, our faces turn red and our knuckles pop. We're so used to strong-arming our way through life's roadblocks that we assume the same style is equally useful in all situations. If a mountain blocks your path, drill your way through it. If a business competitor turns up the heat, bulldoze over him. If an ailment threatens to lay you low, bombard it with drugs and vitamins.

But a simple toy can show us that sometimes our usual strategies of frontal assault and brute strength are self-defeating. They're never more impotent than when used to deal with the distractions we run up against when we try to pray. If we ever hope to make it through the monkey house, we must throw over the urge to do battle and instead take the path of least resistance. There's no way to forcibly rout the monkeys; they'll always be there. But we can learn to ignore their shrieking and hooting. This is what Bosch's Saint Antony teaches us. When we do so, we're able to listen to the secret prayer forever breathing underneath all their racket. And the sound of that prayer—the sound of God—is silence.

Opening Prayer

Quiet the trees; quiet the creepers all.
In the sky's tranquil lap burns the sun's ray.
In my heart's temple doth the silence fall,
Worshipping Thee, Thou, Silent Majestic. Thou
Replenishest this tranquil heart. O Thou
Eternal, Absolute, with silence fill
Me and with song, in secret, silent, still.[3]

Retreat Session Four

Many older hymnals have a section entitled "Christian Warfare." The songs collected there are predictably bellicose. They call us to be soldiers of the cross marching from victory to victory against unnumbered foes ("Stand Up, Stand Up for Jesus"), heroic warriors who fight the holy fight ("March On, O Soul, with Strength"), standard-bearers who enter the fray pealing out the watchword, silencing it never ("Truehearted, Wholehearted"). Probably the most famous of these martial hymns is Sabine Baring-Gould's "Onward, Christian Soldiers," which has us making war against hell's foundations with the cross of Jesus as a battering ram.

Popular as these two-fisted campaign songs may have been in the evangelical nineteenth century, there's something distasteful about them today. Perhaps the experience of two world wars has dampened our enthusiasm for martial imagery; perhaps we've grown ecumenically wary of the "church militant" ideal. Whatever the reason, many modern Christians sense that military metaphors are out of place when we talk about following and serving God.

Nowhere is a martial attitude more inappropriate than when dealing with the monkeys of distraction which stand between us and the secret prayer. The monkeys can't be vanquished by frontal assault. Attacking them head-on in the hope of routing them only dissipates our energy and strengthens theirs. If we pursue them in order to drive them from our minds, we become so caught up in the chase that we run even farther away from the secret prayer. Moreover, we find ourselves in the impossible position of needing to scurry in a thousand different

directions at once. The trees of the mind are alive with
scampering monkeys; they'll always outnumber us.
Finally, we're simply not nimble enough to bag the
monkeys. Just as we think we've got one cornered, it
eludes us and takes off somewhere else.

No, battering rams are useless here. This is what
Bosch's Saint Antony learned. He neither attacks nor
scatters himself in fruitless pursuit. Instead, he sits by the
river and simply ignores the monkeys. They continue
their chattering and shrieking; this, after all, is what
monkeys do. Antony remains aware of their din; how
could he not? But he doesn't allow it to bother him
anymore. He lets the racket slide right over his head
without giving it a second thought. Like his near-
contemporary Evagrios Pontikos, he knows that
inevitably he or she "who practises pure prayer will hear
the demons crashing and banging, shouting and cursing."
They will "suddenly...appear out of the air" to waylay
and frighten. The trick is to "pay no attention to their
threats," to "scorn them utterly."[4] The imps don't quite go
away when we ignore them, but they do cease to distract.

It's significant that Bosch's Saint Antony is seated on
a riverbank. All religious traditions, even those birthed in
arid climates, see flowing water as a metaphor for human
consciousness. The human mind flows continuously. Like
the world's great rivers, it carries along with it a never-
ending flotilla of flotsam and jetsam which so fascinates
us that we rarely make contact with the watery silence
underneath all the traffic. What we must learn to do is
allow anything floating on the river simply to move on.
We shouldn't try to rush it on its course, to control its
movement. All we'll do if we succumb to this temptation
is splash around in the water and make a mess. Ideas,
impressions, memories, desires: let them flow with the
current, let them come and go, and concentrate instead on

the still waters below the surface. This is the trick Bosch's Saint Antony has learned.

The Swiss novelist Hermann Hesse makes the same point in his beautiful novel *Siddhartha*. After a long life of frenetically searching for spiritual enlightenment, the God-seeker Siddhartha wearily settles on the bank of a river and slowly learns the secret of patient listening. At first, all he hears in the rolling water is a deafening cacophony of sounds, echoes of his own troubled spirit. Like Antony, he's tugged this way and that by them; like Antony, his initial impulse is to attack them head-on. But in time Siddhartha recognizes the futility of this approach. In place of it, he ignores the flowing, surface chatter and opens the ears of his heart to what lies beneath it. He ceases chasing first one thought and then the other, redirects his attention, and at last discovers what he longs for. As Hesse says,

> When Siddhartha listened attentively to this river, to this song of a thousand voices; when he did not listen to the sorrow or laughter, when he did not bind his soul to any one particular voice and absorb it in his self, but heard them all, the whole, the unity; then the great song of a thousand voices consisted of one word: Om—perfection.[5]

What Hesse calls "om" our two retreat directors would call the secret prayer, the indwelling Spirit, God within.

Brother Lawrence clearly advocates the spiritual path of least resistance taken by Saint Antony and Siddhartha. "In the way of God," he cautions, "thought counts for little," and this includes the thought-posses we send out to track down outlaw ideas, images and desires. It's much better, says Lawrence, to "[g]ive your attention to keeping your mind in the presence of the Lord. If it wanders and withdraws at times, do not be disturbed. To trouble the mind serves more often to distract than to recall it."[6] Lawrence himself had "reached the point," Abbé de Beaufort tells us, where when temptations threatened his prayer "he sensed their coming, and from the experience he had of God's prompt aid,...he let them advance, and at the right moment called on God. They were gone forthwith."[7] Elsewhere, the Abbé recalled that "[s]ometimes a host of undisciplined thoughts would violently take over the place of God." But instead of attacking them head-on, Lawrence "was satisfied to set them gently aside to return to his customary communion."[8] He sat on the riverbank and let the distractions flow past him.

This strategy of least resistance is also recommended by the unknown author of the fourteenth-century mystical classic *The Cloud of Unknowing*. Like our spiritual directors, the *Cloud's* author was concerned with the cultivation of ceaseless prayer; moreover, he was also well aware of the dangers of monkey mind. He suggests that when we are assaulted by mental distractions during prayer we "must leave them, and put them away deep down in the cloud of forgetting."[9] (A cloud, of course, is simply a river in the sky: mist and water flowing through the air.)

The instruction to sink distractions in a "cloud of forgetting" is intriguing, especially in light of our discussion of "unforgetting" in Day Two's retreat session. The etymological meaning of forget is "to loose or lose one's hold." When we consign monkey-imps to the cloud of forgetting, we open our hands and abandon them. We no longer clutch at them in the vain hopes of shaking them into silence. Instead, we simply let them drift away on the currents of consciousness. When we do so, our spiritual muscles relax. Our unintended, self-hurtful hold on soul-knotting tension and frustration is *lost* when we intentionally *loosen* our hold on combative strategies.

But the monkey-imps of distraction aren't all we abandon when we relegate them to the cloud of forgetting. We also abandon the false self, the willful "me," the ego which resists any diminution of its empire. It only makes sense that the false self likewise sinks into the cloud of forgetting. If the demons of distraction are the soldiers which the false self sends out to defend its sovereignty, it follows that when we forget the distractions we likewise forget the false self. *Forget*, but not *eradicate*. The cloud of forgetting sinks both imps and distractions into a fog which muffles their clamor, but it doesn't destroy them. The monkeys, once again, are always present, even if they're now on the far boundaries of consciousness. Even after we abandon them we still remain peripherally aware of them. The crucial difference, however, is that they no longer hold us.

The abandonment or forgetting of distractions is a necessary condition for awakening to or *un*forgetting the true self, the Christ-self. Brother Lawrence refers to it as a "remembrance."[10] The Pilgrim concurs. When we forget the surface noise of the monkey jungle, he says, we remember the secret prayer and dive deeply to "plumb the depths of [our] own being, to see [ourselves] from within."[11] Even as we loose our hold on irrelevant distractions we tighten our hold on our "own being"—the secret prayer whispered by God. It's only when we make the effort to remember "the depths of [our] heart" that we can "listen carefully to what [the] heart [is] saying."[12]

Heart-listening: this is the core of ceaseless prayer. Scripture is loaded with passages that underscore the spiritual importance of listening. Proverbs tells us to make our ears attentive to wisdom and our hearts to understanding.[13] Jeremiah is wroth against those who have ears but hear not.[14] Jesus several times[15] indicates

that he speaks for those who have ears to listen. Taking
heed of Biblical injunctions to listen, Saint Benedict
famously begins his Rule with this invitation: *Obsculta, o
fili, praecepta magistri, et inclina aurem cordis tui*: "Listen
children to the master's instructions and attend to them
with the ear of your heart."[16] If Benedict is correct, we
listen *to* the heart *with* the heart—that is, we hearken *to*
the secret prayer, the indwelling Spirit, when we respond
to its murmuring *with* our own spirit. Like calls to like,
like listens to like.

But what sense can we make of such spiritual
listening? Lawrence beautifully tells us that it is "an
alertness towards God, a wordless conversation with
him."[17] Compacted in this short description is the great
truth that whatever else spiritual listening is, it is silent.
When we listen, we enter into an attentive
wordlessness—a silence—which in turn "speaks" with
the silence of God. Our silence communes with God's
silence, the holy white noise of Siddhartha's "Om."

Words and language are incredibly useful, but they
tend to get in the way of genuine listening. When the
mind and mouth are full of words, our only desire is to
let them cascade out. We're too busy uttering to harken to
utterances, too preoccupied with what we want to say to
listen to what anyone else has to say. In fact, we
frequently use words that are otherwise quite innocent as
weapons of attack: The more I speak the less you can, and
when I harness you in this way I assert my dominance
over you. The false self goes on the offensive, and the
battering ram it uses is language. Even when there isn't
any apparent intent to dominate, too much chatter can
squander opportunities for genuine heeding.

Scripture is all too aware of our tendency to speak
rather than listen. "I will guard my ways, that I may not
sin with my tongue," the Psalmist writes. "I will keep a

muzzle on my mouth."[18] Proverbs warns us that "[W]hen words are many, transgression is not lacking," and therefore "whoever guards the mouth preserves the soul."[19] The apostle James wonders that such a "small member" as the tongue can do such damage to our souls.[20] Jesus himself cautions us not to "heap up empty phrases," but instead learn to sit still and listen.[21]

If we would listen to the heart's secret prayer, it's necessary, as one recent commentator puts it, to go

> ...beyond thought, beyond concepts, beyond images, beyond reasoning, thus entering a deeper state of consciousness or enhanced awareness that is characterized by profound silence. This is the *silentium mysticum*. It is a state of consciousness in which there may be no words or images.[22]

Scripture as usual puts it more succinctly than theology: "Be still, and know that I am God."[23] When we become silent, we empty ourselves of noise so that we may be totally receptive to the ultimate Reality that underlies everyday noise. We sit in repose, quietly, alertly, heeding with the ears of the heart rather than the intellect, waiting for the still small voice of God. Words are frequently impatient and demanding; silence, on the other hand, possesses the soul in patience. Silence knows how to wait without fidgeting, fully confident that what it awaits is present. "[S]ink down in silence into the depths of [your] heart," advises the Pilgrim,[24] for such a sinking into silence, as Saint Gregory notes, actually "impels our thoughts up toward heaven."[25] Only when one has self-emptied in silence can one "listen carefully to what [the] heart [is] saying."[26]

And how does the secret prayer which is the inner stirring of God speak? What is it that we attend to when we become silent? We attend to divine Silence, for when

God speaks it is the great "Unknown..., hidden in the darkness beyond light," hidden in "mystical silence," who speaks.[27]

The heart, Brother Lawrence says, is a chapel.[28] A chapel is not a stark emptiness or desolate absence. It is an earthly dwelling place of God, filled with the sheer plenitude, the unspeakable fullness, of God's presence. That presence incorporates and goes beyond all words. It is a white noise which rushes in and around us with all the intensity of the eye of a hurricane. John of the Cross more poetically described this white noise as "silent music,...the supper that refreshes," and compares it to "a harmonious symphony of sublime music surpassing all concerts and melodies of the world." This music is silent, he says, "because it is tranquil and quiet knowledge, without the sound of voices."[29] It is the symphonic "voice from heaven like the sound of many waters and like the sound of loud thunder; ...like the sound of harpists playing on their harps,"[30] a harmony so sweetly and encompassingly full that everyday distinctions are lost and the final effect is—Silence. Om. God.

God's silence is the supper that refreshes because it is the source of ultimate repose, of everlasting peace, and it communicates that peace to us, says Brother Lawrence, in "unbroken communion," offering us "grace at every juncture."[31] Lawrence first discovered the silent Presence when he gazed in receptive silence at a winter-blasted tree; the Russian Pilgrim communed with it in the silence and solitude of the Russian steppes and forests. Whenever and wherever it is encountered, the usual worded distinctions with which we carve up and categorize Reality vanish in the mighty and silent rush of the Holy Spirit.[32] We stand before it, opening ourselves to it as a sail opens itself to the ocean breeze, and we are filled with its unimaginable and unsayable power. Our silence embraces divine Silence, and just as a billowing sail cannot be distinguished from the wind that stirs it, so we no longer are distinguishable from the secret prayer, the Christ-self, the eternal Word uttered silently, that blows in and through and around us.

This is what happens when we heart-listen to the secret prayer. This is what it means to practice the presence of God. This is how we forever behold the face of God and therein see our own faces reflected and transfigured. This is how we reach the deification which is our final and best destiny.

Brother Lawrence and the Pilgrim assure us that the monkey-demons can be avoided long enough for us to enter into a silence that communes in prayer with Silence. In tomorrow's session, they make good on their promise by teaching us a concrete and disciplined method for doing so. There's nothing esoteric about their method, nor is it reserved only for saints. It is open equally to all who would pray ceaselessly. It is a gift to each of us, a gift from the silent God.

For Reflection

- *In his Sermon on the Mount, Jesus says that the poor in spirit, the meek, the pure in heart and the peacemakers are blessed. Missing from the list of those who are blessed are "Christian soldiers" who try to assault the monkeys of distraction with energy and brute force. How do poverty of spirit, meekness, purity and peacefulness cultivate the path of least resistance?*

- *When you chase the monkeys of distraction during prayer, what emotions get in the way of your diving to repose? Anger? Frustration? Curiosity?*

- *Why is it so difficult to let the monkeys chatter without trying to chase them down? Could it be a nagging drive to be in charge, to control the situation instead of allowing oneself to be guided by the Holy Spirit?*

- *How long has it been since you were really alert, either in or out of prayer? What was the context of the alertness? What did it "feel" like?*

- *When you wait, are you attentive, or do you squirm? Why?*

- *Many of us find silence uncomfortably threatening, and we do anything we can to protect ourselves from it. We surround ourselves with noise—radio, television, stereo, chatter, print. Why do you think we're so intimidated by silence?*

The silence is all there is. It is the alpha and the omega. It is God's brooding over the face of the waters; it is the blended note of the ten thousand things, the whine of wings. You take a step in the right direction to pray to this silence, and even to address the prayer to "World." Distinctions blur. Quit your tents. Pray without ceasing.[33]

Closing Prayer

In silence
To be there before you Lord, that's all.
To shut the eyes of my body,
To shut the eyes of my soul,
And to be still and silent,
To expose myself to you who are there,
    exposed to me.
To be there before you, the Eternal Presence.

I am willing to feel nothing, Lord,
to see nothing,
to hear nothing.
Empty of all ideas,
of all images,

In the darkness.
Here I am, simply
To meet you without obstacles,
In the silence of faith,
Before you, Lord.[34]

Notes

[1] Hieronymus Bosch's "Saint Antony" is in the Prado, Madrid.

[2] Matthew 7:9.

[3] *The Oxford Book of Prayer*, George Appleton, ed. (Oxford: Oxford University Press, 1989), p. 291.

[4] Evagrios Pontikos, "On Prayer," in *The Philokalia*, Vol. 1, pp. 66-67.

[5] Hermann Hesse, *Siddhartha*, Hilda Rosner, trans. (New York: Bantam, 1981), p. 136.

[6] *Practice of the Presence of God*, pp. 84, 49-50.

[7] *Practice of the Presence of God*, p. 26.

[8] *Practice of the Presence of God*, p. 84.

[9] *The Cloud of Unknowing*, Clifton Wolters, ed. (New York: Penguin, 1970), p. 61.

[10] *Practice of the Presence of God*, p. 73.

[11] *Way of a Pilgrim*, p. 78.

[12] *Way of a Pilgrim*, pp. 78, 20.

[13] Proverbs 2:2.

[14] Jeremiah 5:21.

[15] See, for example, Matthew 11:15, 13:9; Mark 7:35; Luke 14:35.

[16] Timothy Fry, O.S.B., *et al.*, *The Rule of Saint Benedict* (Collegeville, Minn.: Liturgical Press, 1981), p. 156.

[17] *Practice of the Presence of God*, p. 73.

[18] Psalms 39:1.

[19] Proverbs 10:19; 13:3.

[20] James 3:5.

[21] Matthew 6:7.

[22] William Johnston, *Silent Music* (New York: Harper and Row, 1979), p. 55.

[23] Psalm 46:10. The Anglican *Book of Common Prayer* (p. 832) incorporates this line in a beautiful prayer for the gift of silence: "O God of peace, who hast taught us that in returning and rest we shall be saved, in quietness and in confidence shall be our strength: By the might of thy Spirit lift us, we pray thee, to thy presence, where we may be still and know that thou art God; through Jesus Christ our Lord. Amen." I'm grateful to the Reverend Andrew Sherman for bringing this prayer to my attention.

[24] *Way of a Pilgrim*, p. 78.

[25] Quoted in "Ancrene Wisse," in *Anchoritic Spirituality*, Anne Savage and Nicholas Watson, trans. (New York: Paulist Press, 1991), p. 75.

[26] *Way of a Pilgrim*, p. 20.

[27] *The Divine Names and Mystical Theology*, p. 211.

[28] *Practice of the Presence of God*, p. 41.

[29] John of the Cross, "The Spiritual Canticle," in *The Collected Works of St. John of the Cross*, Kieran Kavanaugh, O.C.D., and Otilio Rodriguez, O.C.D., trans. (Washington, D.C.: ICS Publications, 1991), pp. 525, 536.

[30] Revelation 14:2.

[31] *Practice of the Presence of God*, p. 29.

[32] Acts 2:2.

[33] Annie Dillard, *Teaching a Stone to Talk: Expeditions and Encounters* (New York: Harper and Row, 1982), p. 76.

[34] *The Complete Book of Christian Prayer*, p. 12.

DAY FIVE
Heart-reposing

Coming Together in the Spirit

The single-mindedness with which the desert fathers and mothers sought God in the first centuries of Christianity is both a reproach and an inspiration to the rest of us. We're ashamed when we measure our own lukewarmness against their intensity. But we're also reassured that our spiritual lives need not remain tepid. God dwells within our hearts just as surely as He dwelt in theirs. With God's help we can move beyond the false self, just as they did, to embrace the secret prayer that forever whispers in our interior chapel.

Abba Arsenius is a case in point. Born into Roman nobility around 360, Arsenius, like his contemporary Saint Augustine, was one of the best-educated men of his day. But he was no bookish stay-at-home. He knew how to play the worldly courtier, and in quick order was named tutor to the sons of the Emperor Theodosius I. Presumably this appointment was a prelude to higher office. A brilliant career lay before him.

Then the bottom dropped out. In his thirty-fifth year Arsenius appears to have suffered a spiritual collapse (what we today too readily trivialize as "just" a midlife crisis). His vast learning seemed but of straw and his courtly ambitions struck him as ludicrous and hollow. He realized that his mad scramble for recognition and power was taking him farther and farther from where he ought to have been heading. His life, outwardly so successful, was but rust and ashes.

We're told that one night, desperately beseeching God for direction, he heard a voice saying: "Arsenius, flee from men and you will be saved.... Flee, be silent, pray always."[1] This was the breakthrough he'd awaited. The imperial tutor immediately followed the divine summons to throw over privilege and career. He secretly gave his possessions to the poor, sneaked away from the palace, and sailed to Egypt to devote the rest of his life to prayer in the silence and emptiness of the desert. He eventually settled in Scetis and attached himself to the devout hermit John the Dwarf. Abba John gave Arsenius advice he would follow for the rest of his life: spiritual fulfillment comes from being "always mindful of God."[2]

Arsenius became renowned for his holiness, and the desert tradition is rich with stories of seekers who came to him for guidance. The heart of the spiritual instruction he gave them derived from his years with John the Dwarf and can be summed up in two maxims: "Strive with all your might to bring your interior activity into accord with God" and "If we seek God, he will shew Himself to us, and if we keep Him, He will remain close to us."[3] Both of these capture the essence of ceaseless prayer. Perseverance in prayer does not go unrewarded. When we search for God in sincere humility and attentive devotion (when we are watchful, as good Abba John put it[4]), when we still our restless spirit so that it reposes in God and accords with God's will, then God reveals himself to us and abides with us forever. This, Arsenius discovered, is what it means to pray always. It is the good pearl, and we pay but a small price to attain it when we forsake palace and prestige and venture into the desert.

Defining Our Thematic Context

We've reached the point in our retreat where we must follow Abba Arsenius into the silent, empty regions of our hearts. Brother Lawrence and the Russian Pilgrim have helped us make preparations for the journey. With their aid, we've explored the contours of the terrain over which we must traverse as well as the destination. We've discovered that the seemingly distant land for which we yearn in fact is the Kingdom of God that already lies at the core of our being. That Kingdom forever calls to us, promising that if we but dive inwards in prayer, we'll find what we seek.

Our two retreat directors have also forewarned us against the monkey-imps who will try to waylay us as we journey toward the Kingdom. These imps, we've discovered, won't be routed by frontal attacks, but they can be ignored as we silently sink ever deeper into the divine Silence. The trick is to listen so attentively for the secret prayer—to incline the ears of the heart to it, as Saint Benedict said—that we insulate ourselves against irrelevant and distracting buzzing. And when we do that, we achieve the repose of God's presence, "for God is a God not of disorder but of peace."[5]

Our rucksacks are packed and our affairs in order. Now the time has come to stop preparing for prayer and to start doing it. Otherwise we risk falling into the trap of substituting thinking about prayer for actually praying. If this happens, we remain armchair travelers, forever content to read guidebooks about wonderful and marvelous places without ever venturing forth in search of them. So in today's session, Brother Lawrence and the Pilgrim take us by the hand and set out on the trail to the heart-repose which is ceaseless prayer. As in the case of most journeys, the actual travelling isn't nearly as formidable as we might have feared. If we suffer any aches or pains along the way, they'll be tender ones. The yoke is light.

Opening Prayer

> O living flame of love
> that tenderly wounds my soul
> in its deepest center! Since
> now you are not oppressive,
> now consummate! if it be your will:
> tear through the veil of this sweet encounter!
>
> How gently and lovingly
> you wake in my heart,
> where in secret you dwell alone;
> and in your sweet breathing,
> filled with good and glory,
> how tenderly you swell my heart with love.[6]

RETREAT SESSION FIVE

In his Rule, Saint Benedict tells us that if we pray we should do so not with a loud voice but with a silent *intentione cordis*, an inclination of the heart. God is not interested in many words. When it comes to prayer, *puritate cordis*, or an undivided, focused heart, is the goal.[7] Brother Lawrence and the Russian Pilgrim have made it abundantly clear in earlier retreat sessions that they agree with this advice. We must silently and single-mindedly follow our grace-given yearning (recall Augustine's insight about God-desire from Day Two) for the secret prayer if we hope to repose in God. As the Pilgrim says, the point is "to find where your heart is, and to enter it."[8]

But how precisely do we locate the heart's secret prayer in order to repose in it? Our two retreat directors teach a concrete method which Brother Lawrence calls "practicing the presence of God" and the Pilgrim refers to as "self-activating prayer of the heart." Both are identical to what Paul meant by ceaseless prayer.

The beauty of our two directors' technique is that it takes into account our natural preoccupation with wordiness and harnesses it as a vehicle for attaining the silence necessary for listening to the secret prayer. The monkeys of distraction that assail us when we dive—the flood of irrelevant ideas, thoughts, memories and associations—can't be chased out of the mind. But we can begin to redirect our attention from their shrieking by intently focusing on an alternative "noise": what the Russian Pilgrim's hesychast tradition refers to as the "Jesus Prayer." The *starets* who served as the Pilgrim's spiritual mentor describes the strategy in this way:

> The continuous interior prayer of Jesus is a constant uninterrupted calling upon the divine name of Jesus with the lips, in the spirit, in the heart, while forming a mental picture of His constant presence, and imploring His grace, during every occupation, at all times, in all places, even during sleep. The appeal is couched in these terms, "Lord Jesus Christ, have mercy on me." One who accustoms himself to this appeal experiences as a result so deep a consolation and so great a need to offer the prayer always that he can no longer live without it, and it will continue to voice itself within him of its own accord.[9]

The Pilgrim's *starets* knew that fixation on the monkey mind is a difficult habit to break. Like television-viewing, it provides us with entertainment (vapid though it be) while demanding absolutely no activity or effort on our part. We simply sit back and watch, and the more we watch the more passive we become. The only reasonable way to break such an engrained habit is little by little; cold-turkey strategies rarely work for most of us. The purpose of the Jesus prayer is to wean us from passively surfing the monkey-mind by preoccupying us with something else.

Entry into ceaseless prayer, then, makes use of words in order to break our addiction to words. The Jesus Prayer is a mantra which concentrates the aspirant's attention on a short phrase and a mental image until the chatter of the monkeys begins to recede into the background of consciousness. Like all good recovery programs, practice of the Jesus Prayer is progressive: We begin in a self-consciously deliberate way and advance to the point where the prayer takes over and voices itself automatically, "of its own accord." The three stages in this spiritual recovery plan are praying with the lips, praying in the spirit, and praying in and with the heart.

The Pilgrim's own spiritual director started him out slowly but firmly. He gave him a rosary and instructed him to say the Jesus Prayer three thousand times daily, "quietly and without hurry," neither "deliberately increasing or diminishing the number."[10] This is the first step toward heart-repose: mechanically reciting the mantra over and over with one's lips until it becomes such a part of the day's normal routine that when one stops it feels, as the Pilgrim discovered, "as though something were missing, as though I had lost something."[11]

The *starets* gradually upped the ante, increasing the recitations from three thousand to six and finally twelve thousand times a day. Then he gently guided the Pilgrim to the next level: cease saying the Jesus Prayer with the lips and instead utter it mentally—in the spirit—in synchronization with the intake and outflow of breath. When inhaling, silently utter "Lord Jesus Christ"; when exhaling, "Have mercy on me."[12] In this way the prayer is drawn ever deeper into the soul's interior. It ripens from a relatively superficial activity of the lips to the more profound and intimate activity of life-sustaining breath. Instead of remaining on the surface, it begins to flow inside us, inseparably braiding itself into an ongoing process of respiration.

The Jesus Prayer starts at the lips and then sinks to the spirit (*pneuma* means "spirit," but also "breath") But the dive inward doesn't stop here. Once the Prayer has become intimately associated with the sheer act of breathing, it descends yet further, this time into the heart. Here's how the Pilgrim describes this step:

> [L]isten closely to [the heart's] beating, beat by beat.
> When you have got into the way of doing this, begin
> to fit the words of the prayer to the beats of the
> heart one after the other.... Thus, with the first beat,
> say or think "Lord," with the second, "Jesus," with
> the third, "Christ," with the fourth, "have mercy,"
> and with the fifth "on me." And do it over and over
> again. This will come easily to you, for you already
> know the groundwork.... Afterward..., you must
> begin bringing the whole prayer of Jesus into and
> out of your heart in time with your breathing....
> [L]ink the name of God with one's breathing and the
> beating of one's heart.[13]

As we've seen, the technique taught by the Pilgrim's *starets* is one of gradual descent into the profound silence that lies at the core of the soul. By focusing on the Jesus mantra, we're able to deflect the assaults of the monkey-imps. Whenever their shrieking begins to distract, all we have to do is calmly refocus on the prayer and dive deeper, letting their hooting fade into the background. Like Saint Antony and Siddhartha, we simply allow distractions to float past us on the river of consciousness. In the process we so habituate ourselves to a continuous breathing and pulsing of the prayer that it's transformed from an act we self-consciously undertake to an essential and automatic feature of who we are. We replace our habituation to chaotic monkey-mind with habituation to prayerful single-mindedness. And as we sink deeper into prayer we move from a self-consciously worded response to a silent, lived one. As the Pilgrim noted,

> After no great lapse of time I had the feeling that the prayer had, so to speak, by its own action passed from my lips to my heart. That is to say, it seemed as though my heart in its ordinary beating began to say the words of the prayer within at each beat.... I gave up saying the prayer with my lips. I simply listened carefully to what my heart was saying.[14]

It seems as though the heart itself begins to beat the prayer: This is the point where the Jesus Prayer makes contact with the secret prayer in our heart, embraces it in joyful silence and unites with it in active repose. We dive down to the ever-murmuring Holy Spirit, who in turn reaches up to meet us. There's no more separation, no more dissonance, no more noise. The false self has given way to the true self. The busy, fragmented, ever on-the-move ego has "been crucified with Christ; and it is no longer I who live, but it is Christ who lives in me."[15] Because the willful false self has given way to the true Christ-self, what initially called for artifically deliberate effort on our part now becomes effort*less*. Once the Jesus Prayer makes its way down to the silent pulsing of the secret prayer, it becomes "self-activating," self-perpetuating, forever vitalized by its contact with the indwelling presence of God. When this happens, as Saint Hesychios the Priest wrote, we abide in the "stillness" of heart that "breathes and invokes, endlessly and without ceasing, only Jesus Christ who is the Son of God and Himself God."[16] Put a slightly different way, it's no longer we who pray. Rather, the indwelling God prays through us.

If prayer, as Brother Lawrence believes, is the point of contact with God's presence, then continuous heart-repose in that presence is prayer which never ceases. That's why Lawrence says it's impossible to view prayer as a segregated human activity, a mere set-aside time, once we've arrived at the silent unification of our will with God's will. Prayer now is woven into the fabric of daily existence and "the time of prayer [becomes] no different...than any other."[17] Underneath every chore, conversation, or routine the soul "abide[s] in [God's] holy presence," attentively and habitually turning toward "the actual presence of God" in a "wordless and secret conversation ...which no longer ends."[18]

This "unbroken communion" in which we "trust ourselves to God [and] abandon ourselves to Him alone," a communion sustained in love and joy throughout all our daily routines as well as our trials, is Lawrence's practice of the presence of God.[19] To enter into Lawrence's unbroken communion is to discover a world suffused with Spirit. The commonplace is transfigured, and so are we. Pseudo-Macarius, a fourth-century practitioner of the presence of God, put it this way: Unbroken communion means that the prayerful person and God become "one spirit and one temperament and one mind."[20]

The mystical eloquence of Pseudo-Macarius's words ought not lead us to expect that practicing the presence of God hurtles us out of this world into the next. Again, the whole thrust of Lawrence's technique is that it transfigures the commonplace by creating a point of intersection *between* the two worlds. Ceaseless prayer repairs the rupture between the sacred and the secular by enabling us to recognize God's presence even in our most "mundane business."[21] As Lawrence discovered, prayerful mindfulness consecrates any activity—kitchen work, shoe repair, the purchase and transport of victuals—when such "small things" are done in and for "the love of God."[22]

Lawrence's habit of offering up commonplace activities as living prayers is reminiscent of the "little way" practiced and taught by Saint Thérese of Lisieux. Thérese recognized that it's simply not open to most of us to be spiritual heroes of the caliber of a Paul or Catherine of Siena. But all of us *can* work with the spiritual gifts we have, unforgetting God's presence and offering to him the "very little things" we do in our daily lives.[23] The miracle, of course, is that the heart-repose with which we perform such "little things" transfigures them into very big spiritual things indeed. Lawrence and the Pilgrim couldn't agree more.

Three final points should be made before we end today's session:

First, as Pseudo-Macarius reminds us, our resolve to pray must remain constant. Brother Lawrence is probably too autobiographical when he notes that "a *little* perseverance" is initially needed "to form the habit of conversing all the time with God and referring all actions to him."[24] A "little" perseverance may be adequate for someone of Lawrence's spiritual purity, but most of us are so tied to the false self and so addicted to monkey-mind that our progress toward ceaseless prayer will require continuous vigilance and work. Even the Russian Pilgrim struggled for years to make contact with the secret prayer.

It's no good to protest that our everyday lives are too crowded and our responsibilities too pressing to pray much. In the first place, nothing takes precedence over dwelling in the presence of God. What could possibly be more important? In the second place, habituating oneself to the Jesus Prayer doesn't mean removing oneself from the world. As Brother Lawrence has already noted, the whole point of ceaseless prayer is to so integrate it into the warp and woof of one's existence that it becomes a constant companion in all that we do. Reciting the Jesus Prayer is not something we do *apart from* our other activities. Instead, it's the backdrop *against which* we do them.

Second, it ought to be clear by now that neither Brother Lawrence nor the Russian Pilgrim intend to suggest that ceaseless prayer is a hammering at God's door to demand that he reveal himself. Nor do they mean to imply that it's somehow a magical way of invoking God's presence, the rubbing of a genie lamp to release the Holy Spirit. When prayer corrupts to either of these, the egoistically arrogant false self rather than the Christ-self is at work. Instead, our two retreat directors see ceaseless prayer as the opening of our souls to God, a patient waiting for God to come to us. When we pray, we're like the importunate widow in Jesus' parable who sits day after day in the judge's vestibule in the hopes of finally having a word with him.[25] She knows she's powerless to force his hand or dragoon him. So she stills her heart and simply waits. She puts herself at his disposal. She says, "Here I am."

Finally, we should never fetishize the mantra by which we seek entrance into the silence of ceaseless prayer. While it's true that the Greek Fathers placed a high value on the Jesus Prayer taught by the Russian Pilgrim, it's also the case that there are many versions of the Prayer even within the Orthodox tradition. Some are quite abbreviated—"Jesus, have mercy"—while others are almost baroque—"Lord Jesus Christ, Savior and Son of the living God, have mercy on me a sinner." It would be pedantic to insist that one version is more "correct" than others. The actual words used to dive past the monkey-imps into the stillness of God are relatively unimportant; they're the vehicle, God the destination.

Brother Lawrence, for example, was almost certainly ignorant of the Jesus Prayer. But it's clear that the way he trained himself in heart-repose followed the general lines of the Pilgrim's hesychast method. Lawrence told the Abbé de Beaufort that his initial ventures into ceaseless prayer "had used spoken prayer...but afterwards the habit passed."[26] These "spoken" prayers were intentionally short mantras to "keep [the mind] fastened on God alone," and included phrases such as "My God, I am wholy yours," "God of love, I love you with all my heart," and "Lord, fashion me according to your heart."[27] Like the Pilgrim, Lawrence obviously saw the repetition of these worded prayers as method rather than goal.

> After all they are only means to reach the end. Thus, when by this exercise of the presence of God, we are with him who is our end, it is useless to go back to the means. We can continue with him our communion of love, abiding in his holy presence, now by an act of worship, praise, or aspiration, now by an act of self-offering, the giving of thanks, and in all the ways our spirit will know how to devise.[28]

The example of Brother Lawrence as well as of contemplatives before and after him attest to the fact that even though the use of a worded mantra is extremely helpful in our initial forays into ceaseless prayer, the specific content of the mantra is elective. The fourteenth-century author of the *Cloud of Unknowing*, whom we met

in an earlier retreat session, put it well. He reminds us
that what's important in prayer is "a naked intention
directed to God, and Himself alone." In selecting a
mantra, there are no hard and fast formulaic rules. He
says that it's wise to choose a word or phrase short
enough for the mind to retain easily, and that a one-
syllable word such as "God" or "love" is best of all. But
the important thing is to choose one that's meaningful to
you and to "fix [it] fast to your heart, so that it is always
there come what may," a "shield and spear in peace and
war alike."[29]

At the end of the day, Lawrence tells us, our only goal
is silent heart-repose, an abiding in the inner "temple of
the spirit" which allows us to "worship [God]
continually."[30] This, as the Buddhists so wonderfully say,
is the moon. The words we may use to seek admission to
the temple are but pointing fingers.

For Reflection

- *There's a time to think about prayer, and there's a time to
  pray. Instead of reflecting on what we've learned in today's
  session, let's use this time to begin to pray in earnest. Take
  the next thirty minutes or so as an opportunity to start the
  silent dive towards the secret prayer.*

- *Sit in a comfortable position, but make sure your back is
  straight and both feet are firmly on the floor. Relax your
  hands in your lap, close your eyes and take some deep, slow
  breaths. Softly say either the Jesus Prayer or any other
  phrase or word to which you feel connected: "O Lord, come
  to my assistance," "Soul of Christ, sanctify me," "Abba,"
  "Lord, increase my faith," "Speak Lord, your servant is
  listening," "Holy Mary," and so on.[31] It's good to use a
  passage from Scripture, and you might even want to use*

one in Greek, Latin, or Aramaic ("Kyrie eleison," "Veni, Sancte Spiritus," "Marana, tha!") in order to forestall distracting associations with more familiar English ones. Just make sure that the phrase or word you select is brief and simple. It will also probably help to choose one with soft rather than hard syllables.

- *Concentrate on the sound of your prayer mantra as you repeat it slowly and regularly. If it helps, coordinate the mantra with your breathing and use the expansion and contraction of your lungs as an internal metronome. (Don't try synchronizing your mantra with your heartbeat; it's too early for that technique.) If you feel the need to focus on a mental image as well, you may follow the advice of the Pilgrim's starets and imagine Jesus. What may be more helpful at this stage, however, is to imagine yourself peacefully sinking in water, going down deeper and deeper and deeper. As you move steadily into your mantra, you may notice that your closed eyes are beginning to cross. Don't be alarmed. This is perfectly natural.*

- *Whenever monkey-imps begin to pull you away, gently detach yourself from them and unhurriedly turn back to your mantra. Just let the monkeys come and go. They're not your concern.*

- *At the end of your prayer time, offer a short prayer of gratitude for this time you've spent with God and renew your resolve to continue seeking the silence of ceaseless prayer.*

A door opens in the center of our being and we seem to fall though it into immense depths which, although they are infinite, are all accessible to us; all eternity seems to have become ours in this one placid and breathless contact.

God touches us with a touch that is emptiness

and empties us. He moves us with a simplicity that simplifies us. All variety, all complexity, all paradox, all multiplicity cease. Our mind swims in the air of an understanding, a reality that is dark and serene and includes in itself everything. Nothing more is desired. Nothing more is wanting...

You seem to be the same person and you are the same person that you have always been: in fact you are more yourself than you have ever been before. You have only just begun to exist. You feel as if you were at last fully born. All that went before was a mistake, a fumbling preparation for birth. Now you have come out into your element. And yet now you have become nothing. You have sunk to the center of your own poverty, and there you have felt the doors fly open into infinite freedom, into a wealth which is perfect because none of it is yours and yet it all belongs to you.

And now you are free to go in and out of infinity.[32]

Closing Prayer

God of Abraham, God of Isaac, God of Jacob, not of philosophers and scholars.
Certainty, certainty, heartfelt, joy, peace.
God of Jesus Christ.
God of Jesus Christ.
My God and your God.
Thy God shall be my God.
The world forgotten, and everything except God.
Jesus Christ.
Jesus Christ.
Amen.[33]

Notes

1 Benedicta Ward, S.L.G., ed., *The Sayings of the Desert Fathers* (London: A. R. Mowbray, 1975), p. 8.

2 *The Sayings of the Desert Fathers*, p. 78.

3 *The Sayings of the Desert Fathers*, p. 9.

4 *The Sayings of the Desert Fathers*, p. 78.

5 1 Corinthians 14:33.

6 John of the Cross, *The Living Flame of Love*, in *The Collected Works of St. John of the Cross*, pp. 639, 640.

7 *The Rule of St. Benedict*, pp. 255, 217.

8 *Way of a Pilgrim*, p. 88.

9 *Way of a Pilgrim*, pp. 9-10.

10 *Way of a Pilgrim*, p. 13.

11 *Way of a Pilgrim*, p. 13.

12 *Way of a Pilgrim*, pp. 10-11, 37-38.

13 *Way of a Pilgrim*, pp. 90, 164.

14 *Way of a Pilgrim*, pp. 19-20.

15 Galatians 2:20.

16 Saint Hesychios the Priest, "On Watchfulness and Holiness," in *The Philokalia*, Vol. 1, p. 163.

17 *Practice of the Presence of God*, p. 40.

18 *Practice of the Presence of God*, p. 44.

19 *Practice of the Presence of God*, pp. 29, 30.

20 Pseudo-Macarius, *The Fifty Spiritual Homilies and the Great Letter*, George A. Maloney, S.J., trans. (New York: Paulist Press, 1992), Homily 46, p. 231.

21 *Practice of the Presence of God*, p. 27.

22 *Practice of the Presence of God*, p. 23.

23 For her exposition on the "little way," see Saint Thérèse of Lisieux's autobiographical, *Story of a Soul*, John Clarke, O.C.D., trans. (Washington, D.C.: ICS Publications, 1996).

24 *Practice of the Presence of God*, p. 22.

25 Luke 18:1-8.

26 *Practice of the Presence of God*, p. 24.

27 *Practice of the Presence of God*, p. 76.

28 *Practice of the Presence of God*, p. 42.

29 *The Cloud of Unknowing*, p. 61.

30 *Practice of the Presence of God*, p. 61.

[31] These and many other prayer mantras are suggested by Father Thomas Keating in his *Open Mind, Open Heart: The Contemplative Dimension of the Gospel* (Shaftesbury, Dorset: Element, 1993), pp. 134-135, 139.

[32] *Seeds of Contemplation,* pp. 139-140.

[33] Blaise Pascal, *Pensées,* A.J. Krailsheimer, trans. (Hammondsworth: Penguin, 1972), p. 309. The prayer is adapted from Pascal's famous "Memorial," a record of his 1654 unitive experience with God which he wrote immediately afterwards, had sewn into his clothing and wore next to his heart for the rest of his life.

DAY SIX
Living the Prayer

Coming Together in the Spirit

The spirituality of the early Church was in many ways a child of the desert. Abraham and Sarah, the Hebrew prophets, John the Baptist, Jesus: each was tutored by the stillness of its sand and stars. In the first centuries of the new era thousands of God-seekers followed their example, forsaking the company of humans for wilderness solitude. In hearkening to the desert, they not only found the God for whom they yearned. They also discovered a metaphor for the human heart.

At first glance, the desert is an arid landscape utterly devoid of vitality. Nothing can possibly come from its rock and sand save more rock and sand. There's no hospitable greenery in the blazing desert, no promise of growth. So likewise, often, the human heart. Too frequently it strikes us as similarly desolate terrain, a sere, brittle clod incapable of quickening with love or joy or compassion.

But seasoned desert-dwellers know there's another side to the desert. Great promise slumbers beneath its apparent barrenness. Let but a little water fall, and overnight the desert metamorphoses into a succulent garden that welcomes the travel-stained pilgrim and offers a safe haven. So, too, with the human heart. When moistened by the waters of prayer it blossoms into an oasis laden with the fruit of rest and peace.

Saint Hesychios the Priest, a ninth-century desert dweller who was abbot of a monastery at the foot of bleak Mount Sinai, knew as much. In one of the most striking images handed down to us from the desert, Hesychios says this about prayer: "The name of Jesus should be repeated over and over in the heart as flashes of lightning are repeated over and over in the sky before rain."[1] The saint's message is clear: Cultivation of ceaseless prayer heralds a fructification of the heart just as surely as lightning on the horizon signals the rains that transform the desert. Deeply buried potential bursts forth from both, suckled in the one case by rainwater and in the other by the living waters of grace.

John the Dwarf, master of the Arsenius whom we met yesterday, also knew this. The story is told of a wondrous thing that happened to John when he first took to the Egyptian desert in search of God. One day his abba, an old man of great holiness, took a dry stick of firewood, stuck it in the sand and commanded John to water it every day until it blossomed. The well which supplied John and the abba was so far away that it took several hours to go there and return. But John faithfully obeyed his master. Every evening he set out for the well with buckets; every morning he arrived back just in time to water the stick before the sun's blazing heat set in. For an entire year John followed this routine, but the stick remained dead. Another year; again no results. Then came the third year, and the longed-for miracle occurred: The twig sprouted leaves and bore fruit.[2]

The human heart is like John's stick: Even though it can appear lifeless, it carries within it the promise of greenness. When we faithfully water the heart day in and day out with prayer, a miracle happens: The interior

desert blossoms and bears fruit. And as Theodore of
Mopsuestia, another desert saint, said, that fruit is "good
works, love of God, and diligence in the things that
please Him."[3]

Defining Our Thematic Context

The fruit of prayer is a good life, and a good life is
one of loving service to God as well as to our brothers
and sisters. When we embrace the secret prayer, we begin
to *live* it in our daily activities. The practice of ceaseless
prayer rejuvenates our interior life—transforms our
hearts of stone into flesh—and in so doing inevitably
affects our exterior life as well. How could it be
otherwise? "You will know them by their fruits. Are
grapes gathered from thorns, or figs from thistles? In the
same way, every good tree bears good fruit, but the bad
tree bears bad fruit. A good tree cannot bear bad fruit, nor
can a bad tree bear good fruit."[4]

Today Brother Lawrence and the Russian Pilgrim
guide us toward a deeper understanding of what it means
to pray ceaselessly by showing us that genuine prayer
births loving engagement in the world. Their own
experiences attest to the fact that there's no real
dissonance between diving into the silence of prayer and
serving with love amid the world's din. We are not called
to choose between the active way of Martha and the
contemplative (or prayerful) one of Mary.[5] The two paths
converge in ceaseless prayer, and they lead to one and the
same destination: God.

Opening Prayer

God stir the soil,
Run the ploughshare deep,
Cut the furrows round and round,
Overturn the hard, dry ground,
Spare no strength nor toil,
Even though I weep.

In the loose, fresh mangled earth
Sow new seed.
Free of withered vine and weed
Bring fair flowers to birth.[6]

Retreat Session Six

Secular-minded women and men are frequently impatient with the whole idea of prayer. Sometimes this is because they have a chip on their shoulder when it comes to anything that smacks of religion, and dismiss prayer as atavistic superstition. But secular impatience with prayer can also spring from less sour motives. Occasionally it's prompted by an anguished sense of urgency to do something about the palpable injustice that infects society. How in the world can anyone defend wasting time and energy praying when there are so many people who need concrete, this-worldly help? Get off your knees and roll up your sleeves! Do something *really* useful for once!

The assumptions that underlie the secular reformer's impatience with prayer are pretty obvious: Prayer is selfish, prayer is escapist, prayer is useless. It's selfish because the person of prayer is too absorbed with her own spiritual and emotional needs to worry about anyone else. Just look at the Jesus Prayer: It pleads for "mercy on *me*," not "mercy on *us*." Prayer is escapist because the person of prayer distances herself from this world and focuses on the next. Instead of confronting the harsh realities that surround her, she retreats to a comfortable psychological place. Finally, prayer is useless, except maybe as a soothing form of self-hypnosis, because it doesn't get anything done in the real world. Has prayer ever fed a hungry child or taken a homeless person off the streets?

It's all very well to retort that these assumptions are stereotyped or that they misunderstand what's really going on during prayer. But the unhappy truth is that many Christians share them as well, although usually in only an implicit way.

Take my own paternal grandfather, for example. On more than one occasion when I was a boy, Granddad—a laconic Bible-belt farmer—would walk through fields of drought-parched corn and wheat, and sigh: "There's no point praying for rain until the wind changes." What I took then as cracker-barrel humor now strikes me as thinly-veiled cynicism about the "real-world" usefulness of prayer. Without fully realizing it, my grandfather had bought into the secular dismissal of prayer as a waste of time. It simply has no "real world" value.

Then there are those misguided Christians who stoke secular cynicism by using prayer either as a head-in-the-sand strategy for avoiding social responsibility ("I'm not concerned with the passing things of this world. You see, I'm a very spiritual person.") or as an opportunity to drown God in neurotic and utterly self-absorbed supplications ("Just help me out this one time, God, and I'll never ask for anything else!"). We've all run across them, and chances are good we *are* them, at least occasionally. Little wonder secularists snort in impatient derision when they hear the word "prayer."

But these attitudes toward prayer, common as they may be among non-Christians and Christians alike, are quite wrong-minded. Genuine prayer is neither useless nor escapist nor selfish. It's not useless because it bears fruit for both the person who prays and for others. It's not escapist because genuine prayer, authentic prayer, inevitably leads to a fuller engagement in the world rather than a retreat from it. And it's not selfish because the true person of prayer has forsaken the rapacious false self, the whining, demanding ego, for the lovingly generous Christ-self.

Thomas Merton for one warned against confusing the prayerful life with standoffish and self-absorbed escapism. "Nothing is more foreign" to authentic prayer, he insisted, than the assumption that it somehow propels the Christian into a "realm of esoteric knowledge and experience, delivering him from the ordinary struggles and sufferings of human existence." Far from being "a subtle escape," prayer in fact is a "sharing in [Christ's] passion and resurrection and in his redemption of the world." Far from being a strategy for wrapping oneself in "unassailable narcissistic security," prayer "brings us face to face with the sham and indignity of the false self that seeks to live for itself alone and to enjoy the 'consolation of prayer' for its own sake." Far from being a useless form of self-hypnosis, genuine prayer enables us to "listen more intently to the deepest and most neglected voices" in the world around us, and in listening to them reach out to them.[7]

Brother Lawrence and the Pilgrim have already filled in some of the reasoning behind Merton's claims in previous sessions of this retreat. When we move beyond the distractions of the false self, when we silently sink down to secret prayer and hearken to the divine silence that lies at our heart's core, we steadily shed our own will and embrace God's will. We empty ourselves in imitation of the Incarnational self-emptying and make room for God.

But as the apostle John famously tells us, *God is love.*[8] So when we allow ourselves to be filled with God, when we crucify the false self[9] and embrace the Christ-self, we become a new creation,[10] aflame with the very love which is God. It's the nature of love always and everywhere to reach out toward others and serve them with gratitude, humility and compassion. It follows, then, that the more we cultivate ceaseless prayer—that is, the more we attune our will to God's—the more loving our behavior in the world becomes. "Let all that you do be done in love," says Paul,[11] and this is noble, godly advice. But it's only possible after we've learned how to pray.

Prayerfully practicing the presence of God, then, leads neither to selfishness nor escapism, but rather to love. And love in turn is the most powerful force for change in the world because it's a reflection of the awesome power that loved the entire cosmos into existence. Contrary to the cynical viewpoint, nothing could be *less* useless than the love born from and nurtured by prayer.

The mistake we often make is assuming that we somehow must "prepare" ourselves for prayer by first performing good works, that we must wipe our slates clean before we prayerfully present ourselves to God. But this puts the cart before the horse. As the Pilgrim cautions, "thinking that good actions and all sorts of preliminary measures render us capable of prayer" is "quite the wrong way round." In fact, the reverse is the case: "[I]t is prayer which bears fruit in good works and all the virtues."[12] Lawrence agrees. "The practice of God's presence," he tells us, leads to "continual acts of love" and "all the noblest virtues"—not the other way around.[13]

The reason prayer is a necessary condition for genuine virtue is pretty obvious. If we haven't subdued the false self, we risk confusing the egoistic and ultimately self-referential actions it spawns for genuinely virtuous behavior. Humans have an enormous capacity for self-deception, and we're especially clever at coming up with rationalizations that make ourselves look noble. We toss a coin or two at a homeless person huddled over a grate and bask in the glow of our generosity for the rest of the day. We rebuke the teller of a racist joke and walk away with the righteousness of a freedom marcher. We manage an entire day at work without indulging in office gossip and fancy ourselves candidates for sainthood.

Don't misunderstand me. We ought to succor the homeless, oppose racial oppression and avoid idle or malicious chatter. But if we do so only to stoke our egos and feel good about ourselves, we've missed the whole point. We're called to perform such actions out of love for God and others, not love for ourselves. Without the self-emptying, self-giving love which prayer awakens in us— that love which is "the fulfilling of the law"[14]—our "virtuous" deeds ring hollow. As Paul reminds us, "If I give away all my possessions, and if I hand over my body so that I may boast, but do not have love, I gain nothing."[15] The Pilgrim puts it in even starker terms. The person who performs good works out of self-interest—"to be rewarded with the kingdom of heaven"—corrupts himself by attempting to manipulate God. "But God wants us to come to Him as sons to their Father; He wants us to behave ourselves honorably from love for Him."[16]

Paul was savvy enough to recognize how easy it is for even the best of us to confuse self-love with genuine love.

So he provides us with a simple test to distinguish between the two: The more begrudgingly we give ourselves in the service of others, the less genuine love is present. Love "does not insist on its own way," he cautions; "it is not irritable or resentful; it does not rejoice in wrongdoing, but rejoices in the truth. It bears all things, believes all things, hopes all things, endures all things."[17] The genuine love inspired by prayer is profligate. It doesn't hold itself back, nor extend itself in a tentative, testing-the-waters sort of way. Instead, it rejoices in the opportunity to sacrifice itself completely and unreservedly for the sake of the beloved.

Lawrence and the Russian Pilgrim agree that the only way to virtue is through love, and the only way to learn how to love is by making contact with the secret prayer. Too frequently we try to *make* ourselves love in the same way we try to *make* distractions go away: through sheer will-power and frontal assault. This often takes the form of a severe asceticism. We assume that the only way to tame our desires and arrogance is through whipping them into submission.

But ascetic practices alone can't generate virtue. "However much you spend yourself on treating your body hardly," warns the Pilgrim, "you will never find peace of mind that way, and unless you have God in your mind and the ceaseless prayer of Jesus in your heart, you will always be likely to fall back into sin for the very slightest reason."[18] Brother Lawrence concurs. Just as we only exacerbate our distraction by trying to chase down those distracting thoughts, so we distance ourselves even further from love by fixating on "preliminary" ascetic and penitential self-punishments. As Lawrence observed, "one could become entangled in acts of penitence..., leaving love which is the end. This is obvious to see in what people do, and the reason why one sees so little solid virtue."[19] Echoing Paul, Lawrence concludes that "though we should perform all possible acts of penitence, if they were void of love, they would not serve to blot out a single sin."[20]

What, then, is the solution? Prayer. Let go the illusion that good works are a necessary preparation for prayer: "[T]he Christian is bound to perform many good works, but before all else what he ought to do is to pray, for without prayer no other good work can be accomplished."[21] Quit feeding the false self with the stubborn insistence that the soul can cleanse itself on its own steam: Only the "frequent exercise of prayer...recall[s] the soul from sinful action.... Learn first to acquire the power of prayer and you will easily practice all the other virtues."[22] And for goodness' sake, don't mistake the finger for the moon when it comes to ascetic or penitential exercises. As Lawrence told the Abbé de Beaufort, the only good of such exercises is to draw us to God. So why not take "a shorter way" and "go straight there by a continual exercise of love, and doing everything for the love of God"?[23] Don't waste time in preparing to pray: Simply pray. Don't spin your wheels preparing to love: Just love. Don't draw up elaborate blueprints for doing good: Love, and act on that love.

The stick faithfully watered day in and day out by John the Dwarf invisibly and mysteriously quickened on the inside before it burst forth in blossoms and fruit. Something similar happens to us when we water our sere hearts with prayer. An inner transformation precedes and is the immediate cause of observable fruits in our relations with others and God. Our prayerful unforgetting of the secret prayer moistens and vitalizes our spiritual sap, releasing it to flow throughout our entire being.

Brother Lawrence has much to say on the inner quickening brought about by prayer. The practice of

God's presence, he tells us, "produces secretly in the soul wonderful effects," enabling it to labor "quietly, placidly and lovingly before God."[24] The Russian Pilgrim more specifically adds that this interior quickening "bears fruit" in three ways: It purifies the spirit, instilling "love of God, inward peace, gladness of mind"; it gladdens the heart, bestowing on it "lightness and courage, the joy of living"; and it emancipates the mind and will, liberating them from "fuss and vanity" and granting "certainty of the nearness of God and of His love for us."[25] The transfigurative growth within the soul that comes from contacting the secret prayer rejuvenates, in other words, the entire person.

This rejuvenation is possible, Brother Lawrence tells us, because in unforgetting the secret prayer we touch the God who indwells us, and thereby tap into the boundless grace reservoired in the depths of our soul. Prayer is the pump which allows us to draw "in abundance the graces of the Lord." The chief grace to be discovered, as we've already seen, is love, and when we begin to be nurtured by divine groundwater we necessarily imbibe its transformative quality. In it, Lawrence promises, we discover "all virtues though we [ourselves] may lack them all"—which is just to say that the love nurtured by prayer is a surrendering of our will to divine will.[26]

Then the soul blossoms forth for all the world to see. The interior transfiguration leads to overt virtue because our every action, as Lawrence says, is now inspired by the gift of divine love. We recognize in "faith, with love, and with humility" that "our sole business in this life is to please God," and that the way to do this is cooperating with his will to bring about the Kingdom of Heaven.[27] As children of God, created in his image, we are called upon to be co-redeemers of the world, loving it back to its original state of perfection. The twentieth-century

Dominican Gerald Vann recognizes the weight of this privilege and destiny when he writes that

> [T]he world of man is still sunk in sin and ignorance and malice: there is work to be done in the world by those who love God, redemptive work, and for that work God *needs* them.... [T]he more deeply you have become identified with the heart of Christ, the more you will want to help in redeeming creation.... And you can only redeem and restore in the degree to which, being first redeemed and restored yourself, you have learned to love.[28]

And how do we learn to love? Brother Lawrence and the Pilgrim have already made this abundantly clear: by tapping into the infinite Love of the secret prayer. On our own, we are incapable of love, but in the unforgetting of prayer we become charged with it.

And how do we know when we've learned to love? The Russian Pilgrim tells us that the closer our love approximates God's infinite love for us, the nearer we come to the goal. God causes the sun to shine and the rain to fall on the just and unjust alike. Divine love loves all equally. Likewise, we finally shrug off the false self and put on the Christ-self when the secret prayer has become so self-activating that we, too, love all equally. Quoting one of the authors in his beloved *Philokalia*, the Pilgrim insists that "he who has attained to true prayer and love has no sense of the differences between things: he does not distinguish the righteous man from the sinner."[29] Instead, the boundless source of love into which his prayers have tapped flows through him and fountains upwards and outwards to embrace everyone in a profligately generous way. When this happens, we *live* prayer and participate in the redemption of the world.

It's not at all the case, then, that the Jesus prayer's "Have mercy on *me*" is self-absorption. When we ask for mercy, we in effect ask for the grace of at-one-ment with God's will so that we might love and in loving serve others with gladness and singleness of heart. In petitioning God to purify our souls, we do so, as Lawrence says, only so that he may "pour grace on grace" into our hearts until our love becomes a "flowing stream" which rushes forth "wide with force, abundantly," on all humankind.[30]

The twentieth-century Carmelite nun and poet Jessica Powers captures the mystery of prayerful love in one of her most beautiful poems, "I Hold My Heart as a Gourd." The human heart, the heart which has been watered by ceaseless prayer and which has blossomed forth in fragrant and rich fruit, pours out the love given it by God on everyone because it now sees all persons as what they truly are: temples of the Holy, chapels of the living God, sparks of the Divine.

> I hold my heart as a gourd ready to pour
> upon all those who live.
> Not that I see each one as come from God
> and to my soul His representative,
> but that God inhabits what He loves
> and what His love sustains, and hence I see
> in each soul that may brush against my soul
> God Who looks out at me.[31]

To practice the presence of God in ceaseless prayer is to know God as love and to be filled with that love. But it's also to recognize that the entire universe is an outflowing of divine love. God indwells all persons and, once recognized, everywhere invites us to respond to him (them) in love. When we pray authentically, then, we do not forsake the world or cocoon ourselves in protective shells. We throw ourselves into the midst of life, as God himself did at the Incarnation, and gratefully seek to nurture and succor others as we ourselves have been nurtured and succored by a self-giving God. We live prayer, uttering it in our relationships with our individual brothers and sisters, with society and with God Almighty. We experience and celebrate and serve the presence of God in the faces of all persons. This need not mean that we perform deeds which, in the eyes of the world, are "great," but rather that we never miss the opportunity, in whatever "little ways" we can, to live the love prayer has revealed to us. As Lawrence says, God "looks not to the greatness of the deed, but to the love" with which it's performed.[32]

For Reflection

- *Do you really believe in prayer as a vehicle for spiritual transfiguration? Have you ever suspected, even if you've never completely admitted it to yourself, that prayer is just a psychological defense against the harshness of the world? Do you pray in order to console yourself, or do you pray because you long to put yourself totally in the service of God?*

- *It's relatively easy for most of us to sense God's presence in people to whom we're close. But does God brush against your soul when you encounter the homeless? the mentally handicapped? addicts? criminals? irritating coworkers? racists? rebellious teenagers? If not, why not?*

- *Think about Father Vann's claim that we're called by God to be co-redeemers, through love, of creation. In what ways can you participate with this great regenerative plan in your own life? Keep in mind Saint Thérèse of Lisieux's "little ways," mentioned in yesterday's retreat session.*

Mary was praised for having chosen the better part
but Martha's life was useful, for she waited on
Christ and his disciples. Saint Thomas [Aquinas]
says that the active life is better than the
contemplative, for in it one pours out the love he
has received in contemplation. Yet it is all one; for
what we plant in the soil of contemplation we shall
reap in the harvest of action and thus the purpose of
contemplation is achieved. There is a transition from
one to the other but it is all a single process with one
end in view—that God is, after which it returns to
what it was before. If I go from one end of this
house to the other, it is true, I shall be moving and
yet it will be all one motion. In all he does, man has
only his one vision of God. One is based on the
other and fulfills it. In the unity [one experiences] in
contemplation, God foreshadows the harvest of
action. In contemplation, you serve only yourself. In
good works, you serve many people.[33]

Closing Prayer

Lord,
help me be
a soul of prayer;
help me
that all my works
swim in prayer.[34]

Notes

1 Saint Hesychios the Priest, "On Watchfulness and Holiness," in *The Philokalia*, Vol. 1, p. 180.

2 *Sayings of the Desert Fathers*, p. 73.

3 Theodore of Mopsuestia, *Ad baptizandos 1*, A. Mingana, trans., in *Woodbrook Studies* 6 (1933), p. 3; quoted in Boniface Ramsey, O.P., *Beginning to Read the Fathers* (New York: Paulist Press, 1985), p. 169.

4 Matthew 7:16-20.

5 Luke 10:38.

6 *Oxford Book of Prayer*, pp. 88-89.

7 Thomas Merton, *The Climate of Monastic Prayer* (Kalamazoo, Michigan-Spencer, Massachusetts: Cistercian Publications, 1969), pp. 35-36.

8 1 John 4:8.

9 Romans 7:6.

10 2 Corinthians 5:17.

11 1 Corinthians 16:14.

12 *Way of a Pilgrim*, p. 8.

13 *Practice of the Presence of God*, p. 77.

14 Romans 13:10.

15 1 Corinthians 13:3.

16 *Way of a Pilgrim*, p. 34.

17 1 Corinthians 13:5-7.

18 *Way of a Pilgrim*, p. 34.

19 *Practice of the Presence of God*, p. 28.

20 *Practice of the Presence of God*, p. 25.

21 *Way of a Pilgrim*, p. 8.

22 *Way of a Pilgrim*, pp. 170, 9.

23 *Practice of the Presence of God*, p. 25.

24 *Practice of the Presence of God*, pp. 76, 69.

25 *Way of a Pilgrim*, pp. 38-39.

26 *Practice of the Presence of God*, pp. 76, 70, 59.

27 *Practice of the Presence of God*, pp. 42, 51.

28 Gerald Vann, O.P., *The Divine Pity: A Study in the Social Implications of the Beatitudes* (London: Fount, 1985), p. 11.

29 *Way of a Pilgrim*, p. 85. The Pilgrim is quoting Nicetas Stethatus (eleventh century).

30 *Practice of the Presence of God*, p. 36.

[31] Jessica Powers, "I Hold My Heart as a Gourd," in *The Selected Poetry...*, ICS Publications (Washington, 1989), p. 46; quoted in Marcianne Kappes, *Track of the Mystic: The Spirituality of Jessica Powers* (Kansas City, Mo.: Sheed and Ward, 1994), p. 75.

[32] *Practice of the Presence of God*, p. 30.

[33] Meister Eckhart, "Sermon III," in *Meister Eckhart: A Modern Translation*, Raymond Bernard Blakney, trans. (New York: Harper, 1941), p. 111.

[34] *At Prayer with the Saints*, p. 157.

Day Seven
Becoming the Prayer

Coming Together in the Spirit

Here's a story. It comes from one of the apocryphal Infancy Gospels, those wonderful (and sadly neglected) noncanonical narratives of the childhood of Jesus written in the first years of the Church.

One day, when Jesus was about five years old, he wandered down to the stream that ran through Nazareth. He sat by the rushing water and dabbled his toes in its coolness. Then he scooped up a fistful of mud and fashioned the figure of a sparrow. Delighted by his ingenuity, he made another, and then another, until, before long, he was surrounded by a flock of clay sparrows. Then he tenderly cupped one of the figurines in his hands, tossed it heavenward, and *whoosh!*—the mud sparrow quickened with life and soared in the air, chirping gaily and pirouetting with exuberant abandonment.[1]

Now, my guess is that nobody today (and perhaps nobody in the second century, when the tale was first recorded) really believes that this story is *factually* true. I, for one, do not. But exegetical worries about its literal truth are quite beside the point. It is a spiritual story, and like all such stories it conveys a deeply profound meaning that's far more important than whether it is based in fact. The *aletheia* that shines forth from this tale nudges us to unforget something of great significance about our destiny as persons of prayer.

What is it that the story of Jesus and the mud sparrows urges us to recall? Simply—and grandly—this: We who struggle to pray are clay sparrows, weighted down with the mud of our egos, vaguely aware of our true destiny but unable on our own steam to jettison the ballast of our self-will. So the indwelling God, the secret prayer buried deeply within our hearts, takes us into His hands and tosses us into the air. Grace overcomes gravity; our shells split and fall away. At first the acceleration may stun us, and in panic we flap our newly-discovered wings to keep from tumbling to the ground. But then the breath of God catches us and we soar with mounting confidence. As we grow more accustomed to our freedom and lightness, we joyfully embrace what we initially so feared.

The God who molded us out of clay doesn't intend that we should remain earthbound lumps of mud. Our destiny lies elsewhere: in the heavens, soaring ever upwards towards the sun. The ability to take wing is always in us because the same creative God who fashioned us indwells our hearts. When prayer awakens us to His presence, we shake off our torpor and fly: reborn, transfigured, made anew. And in the process, the entire world likewise is transfigured—or, better, we are able to see it for the God-saturated thing it is. A soaring sparrow, after all, takes in more than an immobile clay figurine can.

The story of the boy Jesus gleefully setting free mud sparrows, then, is a parable of the liberation of the human soul. It's also the climax of the story of ceaseless prayer.

Defining Our Thematic Context

Today we reach the end of our retreat with Brother Lawrence and the Russian Pilgrim. But there are two senses of the word "end." On the one hand, it means "termination"; on the other, it means "goal" or "aim" or "culmination." Both meanings are appropriate here. This is the final or terminating session of our retreat, but it's also the day in which our two directors explore the ultimate aim or culmination of ceaseless prayer: that glorious transfiguration in which we no longer *do* prayer but actually *become* it.

Becoming a living prayer, as we briefly saw in Day Two of our retreat, is what the Pilgrim's orthodox tradition calls "deification." In the Carmelite spiritual tradition of Brother Lawrence, it's sometimes referred to as "spiritual marriage." But regardless of the terminology, the idea is the same. As the human soul advances along the path of prayer—awakened by the kairetic opportunity, learning to ignore the monkey-imps of distraction, hearkening to the silence of the secret prayer, attuning its will to the will of the indwelling Spirit, filling and overflowing with love for God and humans—it gradually reaches the point where all the self-imposed barriers that previously separated it from God are removed. At last the soul stands fully and nakedly before the Throne, just as the sparrow flies ever upwards straight into the sun, and the glory of that Throne radiates in and through it.

Then, as Saint Maximos told us, the "participant become[s] like that in which he participates." God so interpenetrates our soul, and the soul so interpenetrates God, that we no longer *practice* the presence of God through prayer. Now we *participate in* the presence of God, joined to the Beloved in the mystical union of spiritual marriage, marvelously deified—made like unto God—by the intimacy of the interpenetration. Like has always called to like. As we've seen, the spark of God which indwells us—the secret prayer—always yearns for a return to the Godhead. Now, in the culminating stage of ceaseless prayer, like returns to like. We no longer do prayer, because the yearning which prompts it is fulfilled. We now *are* prayer: a state of perpetual presence, abiding radiance, everlasting fulfillment. We are sparrows who have flown into the sun, incinerated and yet reborn into our original images by its fiery brilliance.

As the hesychast Theophan the Recluse tells us, "when we receive in our heart the fire which the Lord came to send on earth, all our human faculties begin to burn within," and from this burning "reigns only light."[2]

Opening Prayer

How greatly we rejoice that God indwells our soul!
Even more that our soul dwells in God!
Our created soul is to be God's dwelling place:
and the soul's dwelling place is to be God, who is
    uncreated.
It is a great thing to know in our heart
that God, our Maker,
indwells our soul.
Even greater is it to know that our soul,
our created soul,
dwells in the substance of God.
Of that substance, God, are we what we are!

The Trinity is our Father:
he makes us and preserves us in himself.
The deep wisdom of the Trinity is our Mother:

in whom we are enfolded.
The great goodness of the Trinity is our Lord:
and we are enfolded by him too,
and he by us.
We are enfolded alike in
the Father, in the Son, and in the Holy Spirit.
And the Father is enfolded in us,
the Son too, and the Holy Spirit as well:
all mightiness, all wisdom, all goodness—
One God, one Lord.[3]

Retreat Session Seven

We began this retreat by considering a couple of films
that shed light on inauthentic prayer. Now that we're at
our journey's end, let's examine one more cinematic
image—but one this time that hints at the mystery of
prayer as a sustained way of being.

The film is Martin Scorsese's brilliant interpretation of
Nikos Kazantzakis's novel *The Last Temptation of Christ*.
The particular scene I have in mind focuses on the third
of Christ's wilderness temptations. Satan appears before
Jesus and promises him dominion over all the world, just
as we read in the Gospels. But the Kazantzakis/Scorsese
interpretation adds a fascinating twist to the offer: The
Tempter tries to seduce Jesus by reminding him of a
longing he had as a child. "Remember?" Satan asks.
"When you were a little boy? You cried, 'Make me God,
God! God, make me God!'"[4]

Now, on one level this petition—"God, make me
God!"—can be interpreted as a startling example of
human arrogance run amok. What could be more

presumptuous—more blasphemous—than the human ambition to be on the same level as God? "You shall have no other Gods before me": this is the first commandment.[5] Nor can it be denied that there's merit in such an interpretation. Both Scripture and ordinary experience attest that human pride, the lust to be like God, is an ever-present temptation.

But in every great temptation there's a measure of truth—otherwise the human heart, which after all is innately attuned to God, wouldn't find the temptation so attractive—and the petition "God, make me God!" is no exception. Temptation twists the truth to serve prideful self-will, but nonetheless gestures at a spiritually significant fact. In this case, what's dimly reflected is the intuition that our last and best hope is union with the Godhead. What underlies the apparently blasphemous "God, make me God!" is the heart-deep (even if inarticulate) sensibility that our fulfillment as humans is attained only when we have so aligned our wills with God's that He enters us and we enter Him. "God, make me God!" is, then, really an echo of the secret prayer's "God, take me in! God, let me participate in Your being! God, dissolve the walls between mine and Thine! Pull me into the blazing bush and melt away everything that isn't You!"

This is that longing for the divine interpenetration—the deification—which Maximos and the other Greek Fathers say is stamped on every heart. It's also the essence of the secret prayer. Jesus himself suggests that deification is our destiny when he prays that all humans may be in God "as you, Father, are in me and I am in you...I in them and you in me, that they may become completely one."[6] Paul tells us that to be united with the Lord is to become "one spirit with him."[7] The second Petrine Epistle [8] likewise hints at this destiny when it looks forward to the day when women and men will become *"koinonoi"*—sharers, participants, partakers, partners—of the "divine nature."

The Russian Pilgrim sees the unification of our spirit with God's as the culmination of prayer and calls it "a new birth."[9] It's at this point where prayer crosses over from an activity to a state, from the *attempt to stand before* God's presence to a *continuous presencing in* the Lord. Brother Lawrence refers to this rebirth as an at-one-ment with God, an "unbroken communion," an "abiding in his holy presence," in which the man or woman of prayer "now lives as if there were only God and he in the world."[10] The old person has been forsaken for the love of God and is now "at one with God" even in the smallest and seemingly most insignificant of activities.[11] He or she breathes God, as it were, thinking only of Him, having no will but His, "resolv[ing] to give all for all."[12]

In a pair of passages which are startling not only in their insight but also in their convergence, the Pilgrim and Brother Lawrence focus more closely on what it means to so enter into unceasing communion with God that we become, rather than just do, prayer.

When his *starets* had taught him the method of the Jesus Prayer, the Pilgrim felt the need to retreat into solitude in order to dive more deeply into his heart. After wandering for a time, he came across a deserted hut deep in a forest and spent the next five months there in a "lonely life of prayer." Day in and day out he concentrated on saying, then breathing, then pulsing, the Jesus mantra. By the time he moved on, he had experienced rebirth. As he describes it,

> I grew so used to the prayer that I went on with it all the time. In the end I felt it going on of its own accord within my mind and in the depths of my heart, without any urging on my part. Not only

when I was awake, but even during sleep, just the same thing went on. Nothing broke into it, and it never stopped even for a single moment, whatever I might be doing. My soul was always giving thanks to God and my heart melted away with unceasing happiness.... If I am working at anything the prayer goes on by itself in my heart, and the work gets on faster. When I am listening carefully to anything, or reading, the prayer never stops; at one and the same time I am aware of both.[13]

The parallel passage from Lawrence comes to us from the Abbé Beaufort's recollections. After describing Lawrence's attempts to practice the presence of God, the good abbé says this:

Finally his faithfulness won the reward of an unbroken remembrance [that is, an unforgetting] of God. His many and varied doings were changed into a simple vision, an enlightened love, an unbroken enjoyment. As he would say: "The time of action does not differ from that of prayer. I possess God as peacefully in the bustle of my kitchen, where sometimes several people are asking me for different things at the same time, as I do upon my knees before the Holy Sacrament. My faith even becomes so enlightened that I think I have lost it. It seems to me that the curtain of obscurity is drawn, and that the endless cloudless day of the other life is dawning."[14]

There are at least three points made by the Pilgrim and Lawrence worth noting here. The first is that when we move from doing to becoming prayer, we no longer draw distinctions between sacred time and secular time. Presencing in God is not an activity that somehow gets sandwiched between all our other activities. Instead, it becomes a permanent state that continues regardless of whether we're awake or asleep, on our knees or engaged in the hustle and bustle of mundane affairs. Both of our retreat directors underscore this by speaking of the presencing's "unbrokenness." Put a slightly different way, the present coincides with the Presence: At any given moment, in any given activity, prayerful interpenetration with God *is*. The ordinary is transfigured, the commonplace sanctified.

The second characteristic of becoming ceaseless prayer follows closely from the first: It's as effortless as the pulsing of our hearts or the breathing of our lungs. *Doing* prayer requires resolution and discipline. If there's anything that our earlier retreat sessions have shown us, it's that getting started in prayer can be an arduous undertaking, in spite of the fact that we're naturally inclined to it. But once we've dived, by-passed the distractions, and made contact with the secret prayer— once we *partake* of the Presence in the present—the struggle is over. There's no question now of striving to pray, of toiling to overcome the false self for the sake of the Christ-self. The indwelling Spirit's continuous murmuring of the secret prayer takes over. The prayer, to use the Pilgrim's expression, becomes "self-activating"; Lawrence means the same thing when he tells us that it becomes "natural."[15] And when this happens, the resisting heart of stone melts. "Faith," the conscious and deliberate effort to remain loyal to God, becomes so "enlightened" that it passes away. What need is there of faith in things unseen when we have immediate and continuous experience of them?

Finally, both the Pilgrim and Brother Lawrence concur that when we cross the threshold from doing to becoming prayer, our lives are suffused with a rich sense of fulfillment. We experience "unceasing happiness," "unbroken joy." How could we not? Our heart's deepest yearning is now satisfied. That for which we are destined—the active repose of loving communion with the source of all love—is achieved. Brother Lawrence speaks of this fulfillment in a particularly tender way. The image he appeals to is reminiscent of the maternal language the good and holy Dame Julian of Norwich used in the fourteenth century when she wrote of divine love. Here's what Lawrence says:

> My commonest attitude is this simple attentiveness, an habitual, loving turning of my eyes to God, to whom I often find myself bound with more happiness and gratification than that which a babe enjoys clinging to its nurse's breast. So, if I dare use this expression, I should be glad to describe this condition as "the breasts of God," for the inexpressible happiness I savor and experience there.[16]

We learned in yesterday's retreat session that prayer is neither useless nor escapist. When we begin to live prayer, we experience an interior transformation that necessarily leads to an external one as well. The Christ who indwells us fills us with such an abundance of love that it overflows into our relations with our sisters and brothers. When we gaze into their faces we see God, and yearn to serve him by serving them.

The culminating stage of this transformative process occurs when we move from living to becoming prayer. We've already seen that an unbroken communion with God eliminates the false distinction between sacred and secular time. But it also dissolves the equally spurious one between sacred and secular place. In entering into ceaseless prayer, we forsake a world comprised of nothing but inert, physical objects and impersonal natural law. Now we see the earth and all its resources through God's eyes, as it were, and they reveal themselves as the

God-saturated wonders they are. Just as God indwells all humans, so He likewise indwells creation as a whole. "The earth is the LORD's, and all that is in it."[17] God's holiness surrounds us. It's the ocean in which we swim, the air we take into our lungs. We are no longer strangers in a strange land.

The Pilgrim is especially struck by the way ceaseless prayer reveals the ubiquity of God's shining presence. He tells us that when he reached the point of sustained prayer, "[T]he whole outside world...seemed to me to love and thank God: people, trees, plants, and animals. I saw them all as my kinsfolk; I found on all of them the magic of the name of Jesus."[18] When he prayed, he says, "[E]verything around me seemed delightful and marvelous. The trees, the grass, the birds, the earth, the air, the light...witnessed to the love of God..., all things prayed to God and sang His praise."[19]

Our two retreat directors lived, of course, in an age largely innocent of our present ecological concerns. But their experiences of prayerful communion with God anticipate the insight to which we contemporary Christians are slowly and painfully making our way: that the earth, the physical cosmos, is part of the body of God, shot through and through with divine Presence and hence worthy of our praise, our wonderment and our care. To honor and love God's creation is to honor and love God. This is one of the insights we absorb when we become prayer, and it affects our comportment in the natural world just as surely as our living the prayer affects our relations with other people. No, prayer is neither useless nor escapist. It's the catalyst, as Father Vann told us in Day Six, for growing into our responsibilities as co-redeemers of creation.

We're in a better position today to grasp more fully what Vann means when he talks about our roles as praying co-redeemers. Look at it this way: Because God is the gracious and loving Creator of all that is, his presence always and everywhere permeates reality. But there's also separation between creation and Creator. Human willfulness—mythically symbolized for us in biblical stories such as the Edenic expulsion, the tower of Babel, and the great flood—has ruptured the original integrity of the cosmos, and this rebellion distances not just humans but, somehow, creation itself from its sustaining source. That's why Paul writes that *all* creation—human as well as natural reality—groans and travails for reunion with God.[20]

Since the proper destiny of all creation is to abide in God, it's the responsibility of humanity—that part of creation most in the likeness of God—to struggle to overcome the breach. But as we've seen, we can do so only when the false self has been subdued and we grow into and embrace the Christ-self. Unification, the interpenetration of God and humans achieved when we become prayer, purifies our will by bringing it into full accordance with God's. Since his will is now ours, divine love can work in and through us to heal the rupture between creation and Creator. We are co-redeemers because we make ourselves instruments of the Lord. We become the hands of the supreme Artisan, guided by his will, moving by his inspiration.

The *Zohar*, a thirteenth-century classic of Jewish mystical prayer, shares this intuition. It tells us that the ultimate end of each human being is *devekut*, a prayerful cleaving to God analogous to Saint Maximos's notion of deification. When *devekut* is achieved and the rupture between humans and God repaired, then the person of prayer co-participates in *tikkun*: cosmic restoration. Our ceaseless prayer is itself an act of *tikkun*, but other *tikkunim* include works of charity, love and compassion for all of God's creation. In becoming prayer, we also become restorers. In presencing God, we help God become all the more Present to the world.[21]

Saint Paul—the same Paul who urges Christ-followers to ceaseless prayer—puts the same point in a different way. In his Second Letter to the Corinthians he tells us that whoever is "in Christ" (or cleaves to God) becomes a "new creation."[22] Paul is gesturing here at the mystery of unification: We are "in Christ" when we so embrace God's will that we become prayer. But Christ came to reconcile the world to God. Consequently, to embrace God's will is to continue God's work of reconciliation or restoration (*tikkun*), and this means that "we are ambassadors for Christ, since God is making his appeal through us."[23]

Now, Paul's use of the word "ambassador" is particularly revealing. The Greek is *presbeutes* (the Latin is *legatus*), a legal and political term with two interrelated meanings. The first suggests that a *presbeutes* has a direct commission from whomever he or she serves; the second, that a *presbeutes* is responsible for bringing others into the service of his or her master. Both of these functions are part and parcel of the new birth that occurs when we become prayer. We have a direct commission from God by virtue of our unbroken communion with him, and that commission is to participate in his work of cosmic restoration by praying/loving the world back into unity with its source. This "ministry of reconciliation"[24] is Godlike work, and when we accept it we come into our own as Godlike creatures.

At the end of the day, this is what ceaseless prayer is all about: returning to the source whence we came, and in the process drawing all of creation with us. God "greatly desires to make us like him if we will," says Lawrence. "Who will be so unwise as to turn away, even for a moment, from the honor, from the love, the service and the unending worship that we owe to him?"[25] So "let us return to ourselves"—our *true* selves, our Christ-selves—that we may dwell in that ever-active repose which is ceaseless communion with God. Help us, O God, to become *koinonoi*, participants in you and your plan. God, make us God. And let it be soon; for, as Lawrence tells us, "Time presses."[26]

For Reflection

- The third-century Greek Father Origen says that we ought to think of the whole of Christian existence as a "single great prayer."[27] What thoughts does this bring to mind on what it means to be a Christian?

- In Day Two of our retreat, we considered what "active repose" in God might be like. Return to the same question now, reexamining it in light of today's retreat session.

- In meditating on his own journey toward God, Brother Lawrence has this to say: "Sometimes I think of myself as a piece of stone before its sculptor, from which he intends to make a statue. Setting myself thus before God, I beg him to shape his perfect image in my soul, and to make me exactly like him."[28] What's the nature of the stone the divine sculptor must chip away in order to invite your soul to become prayer?

- Think about the meaning of tikkun. What tikkunim do you feel called to? Why?

- All of us, surely, have had glimpses of the transfigured natural world about which the Pilgrim so eloquently writes. Reflect on your own experiences of a world in which "people, trees, plants, and animals" pray to God *and sing his praise.*

- *When we become prayer, the present becomes Presence.
  Explore your reactions to this claim. What implications
  does it have for our sense of time? our worldly aspirations?
  our individual identities?*

- *"Time presses," warns Brother Lawrence. But what does he
  mean? Obviously one interpretation is that life is short,
  and so opportunities for the cultivation of prayer ought not
  to be neglected. But there are numerous other meanings
  Lawrence probably intends here as well. What are some of
  the ones that come to mind?*

[A] baby, even though it is powerless to accomplish
anything, or with its own feet to go to its mother,
still rolls and makes noises and cries, as it seeks its
mother. And the mother takes pity on it and is glad
that the baby seeks after her with pain and
clamoring. And though the baby is unable to come
to her, because of the child's eager searching, the
mother comes to it herself, all out of love for the
baby. And she picks it up and fondles it and feeds it
with great love. This also is what God, the Lover of
mankind, does to the person that comes to him and
ardently desires him. But there is even more.
Impelled by love, he himself, by the goodness which
is inherent in him and is all his own, enters with that
person "into one spirit," according to the apostolic
saying. When a person clings to the Lord and the
Lord has pity and loves him, coming and clinging to
him, and he has the intention thereafter to remain
constantly in the grace of the Lord, they become one
spirit and one temperament and one mind, the
person and the Lord.[29]

Closing Prayer

Be joyful always.
Know that God's Presence is with you,
that you are looking directly at your Creator
and your Creator at you.
Know that the Creator can do all that He desires:
that in an instant
He could destroy all the worlds,
and in an instant renew them.
In Him are rooted all powers, both good and harmful;
His flowing life is everywhere.
Only Him do I trust!
Only Him do I fear![30]

Notes

[1] "The Infancy Gospel of Thomas," in *The Other Bible*, Willis Barnstone, ed. (San Francisco: Harper, 1984), p. 399.

[2] *The Art of Prayer*, p. 156. Theophan is paraphrasing the sixth-century Palestinian Saint Barsanouphios.

[3] Julian of Norwich, *Revelations of Divine Love*, Clifton Wolters, trans. (New York: Penguin, 1966), pp. 157-158.

[4] For the parallel passage in Kazantzakis's novel, see *The Last Temptation of Christ*, P. A. Bien, trans. (New York: Bantam, 1968), p. 256.

[5] Exodus 20:3.

[6] John 17:21, 23.

[7] 1 Corinthians 6:17.

[8] 2 Peter 1:4.

[9] *Way of a Pilgrim*, p. 181.

[10] *Practice of the Presence of God*, pp. 29, 40, 74.

[11] *Practice of the Presence of God*, p. 27.

[12] *Practice of the Presence of God*, p. 56.

[13] *Way of a Pilgrim*, pp. 39-40.

[14] *Practice of the Presence of God*, p. 84.

[15] *Practice of the Presence of God*, p. 57.

[16] *Practice of the Presence of God*, p. 45.

[17] Psalm 24:1.

[18] *Way of a Pilgrim*, p. 93.

[19] *Way of a Pilgrim*, p. 30.

[20] Romans 8:22.

[21] *Zohar: The Book of Enlightenment*, Daniel Chanan Matt, trans. (New York: Paulist Press, 1983). For a discussion of *tikkun* in the context of Jewish mystical prayer, see Dan Cohn-Serbok & Lavinia Cohn-Sherbok, *Jewish and Christian Mysticism: An Introduction* (New York: Continuum, 1994), chapters 1-4.

[22] 2 Corinthians 5:17.

[23] 2 Corinthians 5:19, 20.

[24] 2 Corinthians 5:18.

[25] *Practice of the Presence of God*, p. 71.

[26] *Practice of the Presence of God*, p. 36.

[27] Origen, "On Prayer," in *Origen*, Rowan A. Greer, ed. and trans. (New York: Paulist Press, 1979), p. 104.

[28] *Practice of the Presence of God*, p. 46.

[29] Pseudo-Macarius, *The Fifty Spiritual Homilies and The Great Letter*, Homily 46, p. 231.

[30] Zawa'at RIVaSH 18a; quoted in *Your Word Is Fire*, p. 81.

Deepening Your Acquaintance

■ Even though there are various editions of Brother Lawrence's and the Russian Pilgrim's books, there's a curious paucity of secondary literature on them (and particularly on the Pilgrim). But for readers who wish reliable translations as well as historical and theological commentary, two recent critical editions may be helpful. Both volumes have fine introductory essays and bibliographies.

Aleksei Pentkovsky, ed., and T. Allan Smith, trans., *The Pilgrim's Tale* (New York: Paulist Press, 1998).

Salvatore Sciurba, O.C.D., ed., *The Practice of the Presence of God* (Washington, D.C.: ICS Publications, 1994)

■ For background on Brother Lawrence's tradition of Carmelite spirituality, no better resources could be suggested than the works of Teresa of Avila and John of the Cross. Teresa, especially, is accessible to a general audience, while John is a bit more labor-intensive. The Institute of Carmelite Studies publishes (at quite reasonable prices) the complete works of each:

The Collected Works of St. John of the Cross, 1 Volume, Kieran Kavanaugh, O.C.D., and Otilio Rodriguez, O.C.D., trans. (Washington, D.C.: ICS Publications, 1991).

The Collected Works of St. Teresa of Avila, 3 Volumes, Kieran Kavanaugh, O.C.D., and Otilio Rodriguez, O.C.D., trans. (Washington, D.C.: ICS Publications, 1980-1987).

■ Commentary on Teresa and John abounds, but one of the most exhaustive and convenient is:

E. W. Trueman Dicken, *The Crucible of Love* (New York: Sheed and Ward, 1963).

■ The hesychast spiritual tradition is as rich in literature as the Carmelite one. Absolutely indispensible is the *Philokalia*, that collection of fourth- to fifteenth-century orthodox texts so loved by the Pilgrim. A modern translation of it, in four volumes, is available:

The Philokalia, G. E. H. Palmer, Philip Sherrard, Kallistos Ware, eds. (London: Faber and Faber, 1979).

■ Hesychast writings from the modern era are collected in an equally valuable volume cited several times in this book:

Timothy Ware, ed., *The Art of Prayer: An Orthodox Anthology* (London: Faber and Faber, 1966).

■ Also worth consulting are two books on prayer written by orthodox priests:

Anthony Bloom, *Beginning to Pray* (New York: Paulist Press, 1970).

Ignatius Brianchaninov, *On the Prayer of Jesus*, Father Lazarus, trans. (Shaftesbury, Dorset: Element, 1993).